Marga Biazzi · Paolo Bertazzo

YŌKAI TAROT

The Deck of Japanese Folklore

LO SCARABEO

Marga Biazzi · Paolo Bertazzo

YŌKAI TAROT

Art by Marga Biazzi
Text by Paolo Bertazzo

Graphic Design by Chiara Demagistris
Translations by Emily Guidoni,
María Victoria Filadoro, Alessia Casciaro
Editing by Paolo Bertazzo, La Forgia dei Libri

Printed by Imago Publishing Limited
in December 2024

Lo Scarabeo
Via Cigna 110 – 10155 Torino – Italy
info@loscarabeo.com – www.loscarabeo.com
Facebook & Instagram: loscarabeotarot

TABLE OF CONTENTS

YŌKAI TAROT

INTRODUCTION

Up on the snow-capped brims of the volcanos, or deep down in the turbid waters of the Pacific; hidden in cold, hollow caves in the ground, or sheltered below the thick canopy of the forests; fluttering idly with the cherry petals, carried by the tepid winds of spring, or concealed among the knickknacks in the darkest, most secluded corners of your attic—any place you can think of may be the home of a *yōkai*, one of the spirits of Japanese folklore.

These creatures have populated the Land of the Rising Sun since its glorious dawn, when *Izanagi* himself raised it from the ocean's depth by churning with the tip of his legendary jeweled spear. From time immemorial, they have lived alongside Men, sharing Earth and its events, appearing seldom and when least expected—an erratic behavior inferred by the term *yōkai* itself, usually translated as "strange apparition," despite the fact that both of the *kanji* used to write it (妖怪) actually bear the same meaning: "suspicious," "dubious," and "mysterious."

Those who are not familiar with the *yōkai* tend to approach them as an exotic collection of fantasy beasts, ghosts, and gods—but nothing could be further from the truth. As a matter of fact, these beings are an integral part of Japan's cultural heritage, sprouting directly from its indigenous religion, Shinto, which holds the animistic belief that all things in Nature (and even certain objects) possess a soul. The result of this conviction is a world filled with essence, sentience, and meaning, a world in which anything has agency and will, and can therefore be interacted with directly.

In short, the *yōkai* represent the personification of all phenomena of reality—and consequently, knowing how to deal with them means to know how to deal with reality itself.

With this in mind, the union with a tool of inquiry and self-reflection like Tarot appears as obvious and natural as ever, as it defines the point of connection between two complementary mechanisms: the manifestation of the world as an immanent interlocutor and the communicative power of the 78 Arcana to initiate a dialogue with it. Yōkai Tarot is the result of this unique combination.

HOW TO USE THE DECK

Using the Yōkai Tarot deck means to set off for an adventure across the enchanted lands of ancient Japan, from the warm, tropical beaches of Kyushu in the southwest, to the frozen forests of Hokkaido at the northeastern corner of the archipelago.

Of course, as any adventure worthy of the name, there is no single road for you to take, but a myriad of different paths to choose from, depending on the quest you want to pursue. In the context of the Yōkai Tarot, each of these paths is metaphorically represented by a Spread—that is, the way in which Tarot cards are laid out when drawn to perform a reading. Each card occupies a particular position in this sequence, symbolizing a specific step in the adventure, which the corresponding Arcanum will describe and interpret.

As a matter of fact, any Arcanum drawn from the Yōkai Tarot deck represents a sudden encounter with a spirit, creature, or *kami* along the path described by your Spread. This apparition can be pleasant or ominous, soothing or cathartic—but one thing is certain: it will be purposeful, as it will guide you along this journey.

SPREADS

There are countless Spreads available. Some are classic Spreads, commonly used with any Tarot deck, while others are unique to the deck they have been developed for. Below you will find a list of Spreads, arranged in ascending order of complexity. Feel free to develop your own personal Spread according to your needs.

A CARD A DAY

1

A Card a Day is the perfect method to summon a quick burst of inspiration to guide you through the day. Turn to this method right after wake-up, so as to get immediate direction on the hours ahead of you. To perform the *A Card a Day* Spread, draw a card. Look at the artwork, then read the keywords and the description in the booklet. Meditate on those words and keep them in mind throughout the day, taking advantage of the message whenever it applies.

THE THREE-CARD SPREAD

The *Three-Card Spread* is one of the most popular Spreads in the Tarot world, and it works best as a direct response to a specific question. This simple sequence allows for a number of interpretations, and the one to use should be decided in advance, depending on the pattern that best suits the question in place. To perform the *Three-Card Spread*, formulate a question, establish which interpretative key you will apply to this Spread, then draw three cards and lay them out in front of you as shown in the image above. Look at one card at a time, and consider how each meaning relates to the role assigned by the corresponding position in the Spread. Once you have analyzed each Arcanum individually, you might also draw conclusions from the order in which they appeared, and the message embedded in the sequence.

1: Past | **2**: Present | **3**: Future

1: Person 1 | **2**: Person 2 | **3**: Common ground

1: Goal | **2**: Obstacle | **3**: Help

THE TORII SPREAD

This unique Spread, designed specifically for the Yōkai Tarot, takes the shape of a *torii* (鳥居, literally: "bird perch"), the famous ceremonial gates found at the entrances of Shinto shrines. The *torii* represents a threshold between the earthly and spiritual realms, and as such it introduces the reader toward higher levels of consciousness. This Spread ought to be used specifically as a guide for your meditation: build your *torii* piece after piece in order to walk through it and achieve enlightenment. To perform the *Torii Spread*: Draw six cards, then lay them out in front of you as shown in the image above. Starting from the bottom layer, meditate on the pictures and stories of the *yōkai,* and the meanings of the corresponding Arcana in relation to the position they occupy in the Spread's structure. In doing this, consider both cards separately, or combine them to narrow down the scope of your meditation. Once you are satisfied with the results, proceed upward to the layer above—but make sure never to advance beforehand! The *torii* will crumble if the underlying levels have not settled, preventing you from completing the gate and traversing it to transcend your current state of mind.

1-2: The principles at the base of your journey; the underlying values that must guide your every step. These foundations will bear the weight of all that is coming, serving as the conceptual tenets of this new structure.

3-4: What you need to let go to proceed; episodes, people, or concepts that can now be settled upon the pillars of truths you have just erected. What were once considered burdens must now be overcome and "laid down," turned into experiences to create a new stability to build upon. The release makes you light and free to ascend.

5-6: The epiphany at the end of your journey; the turning point of your consciousness. Your newfound values have allowed you to release earthly matters; and in release, those matters have turned into lessons. Your mind is ready to soar among these heavenly truths and grasp them to complete the evolution of the self.

CARDS

Tarot cards are called Arcana. There are 78 of them in total, divided between Major and Minor Arcana. Each Arcanum displays a particular *yōkai* in the guise of the corresponding Tarot archetype. The following instructions present a set of useful keywords describing the general concepts tied to each Arcanum, but also include a description of the specific *yōkai* and how it relates and expands on the archetype it represents. You can decide whether to consider just the traditional themes of the keywords or the whole story and explanation of the *yōkai*—or even a combination of the two—when interpreting the meaning of your Spread.

MAJOR ARCANA

The 22 Major Arcana—listed with Roman numerals, from 0 to 21—are the most important cards in a Tarot deck. Sometimes called Trumps (or Triumphs), they represent powerful concepts and archetypes, overarching themes and ideas with broader implications and a more general scope.

0 · THE FOOL — *Keywords: Freedom, Spontaneity, Innocence, Madness, Naivety.* The *kappa* (河童, literally: "river child"), a water *yōkai* living at the bottom of ponds and rivers, is one of the most popular creatures of Japanese folklore. Upon its head is a depression called *sara* (dish) filled with water, and it is believed that if the liquid is spilled, the *kappa* loses all its energies. So, in order to keep the water in, the *kappa* must always walk with its head held high: this allows it to have great vision, but prevents it from seeing what is below its very feet. As you can see, adventure can be both liberating and perilous, so enjoy it with caution!

I · THE MAGICIAN — *Keywords: Will, Ability, Ambition, Trickery, Deception.* One of the most iconic *yōkai*, the *bake-danuki* (化け狸, literally: "changed raccoon") is a supernatural being with the looks of a Japanese raccoon dog and incredible shape-shifting powers, which it employs to fool travelers for the sake of a good laugh. This spirit's tricks and disguises represent great skill and versatility, as well as mastery over the emotional, intellectual, material, and creative realms, symbolized by the four Suits depicted in the artwork. Pursue your projects and perfect your many talents, but remember to eventually settle on a form, or you will lose track of who you truly are.

II · THE HIGH PRIESTESS — *Keywords: Wisdom, Intuition, Secrecy, Introspection, Severity. Yuki-onna* (雪女, literally: 'snow woman") is a spirit of ice and cold, manifested under the guise of a young and beautiful lady. She is said to appear during heavy snowstorms, preying on lost wanderers. She often leaves the traveler frozen in the snow; however, some instances have been recorded of her helping men with information on how to get out of the blizzard. The ways in which the *yuki-onna* dispenses her wisdom are ambiguous and cryptic. Accept them as they come, trusting that forces are at work to direct your path. Exercise your intuition to detect the signs.

III · THE EMPRESS — *Keywords: Abundance, Fertility, Elegance, Beauty, Protection.* The story of *Kaguya-hime* (かぐや姫, "princess Kaguya"), the girl from the moon who was discovered by a bamboo cutter inside a shining stalk, is one of the oldest of Japanese folklore. Before returning to her home in the sky, she made the finder rich and gave an elixir of immortality to the emperor of Japan, but the sovereign destroyed it, for he did not wish to live for eternity without her. That of *Kaguya-hime* is a tale of love, purity, and a great sense of belonging—all the qualities of the Empress. It represents plentitude and fecundity, but also the nobility of spirit to give all of that away to others' benefit.

IV · THE EMPEROR — *Keywords: Power, Authority, Discipline, Experience, Precision. Ryūjin* (龍神, literally: "dragon god"), king of the sea and patron of Japan, dwells in *Ryūgū*, the underwater palace built into a coral reef. From the rooms of this mansion, the dragon god reigns over his fish servants, bringing storms and thunders to the world above the surface, and controlling the tides with the magical jewels in his possession. His appearance urges you to assert yourself: take the situation into your hands, and control it; establish some boundaries, and defend them. However, make sure to be respected rather than feared—severity and cruelty are two very different things.

V · THE HIEROPHANT — *Keywords: Knowledge, Inspiration, Faith, Conformity, Hierarchy.* Turned into a man by its shapeshifting powers, this *bakeneko* (化け猫, literally: "changed cat") has devoured a monk to take his place as the keeper of the temple. Don't misinterpret this act as a mere trick or a joke, because this feline spirit acts with a purpose—whether it is to manipulate and control, or to guide and conform, is for you to discover. Look deep into the situation, because there might be more than meets the eye. It is not wrong to follow the tradition and find a place into society, but make sure not to lose your true identity when trying to blend in.

VI • THE LOVERS — *Keywords: Joy, Passion, Union, Desire, Choice.* When the goddess *Orihime* (織姫, literally: "weaving princess") fell in love with *Hikoboshi* (彦星, literally: "star boy"), her father *Tentei* forbade her to cross the Milky Way to meet him, as he worried that she would abandon her duties for him. Moved by his daughter's tears, *Tentei* subsequently allowed them to meet, but only once each year, on the seventh day of the seventh month, when a flock of magpies would make a bridge with their wings to reunite the couple. This episode speaks of unbridled desire, a longing for the other, but it also refers to the sacrifices that must be made to establish a meaningful connection. When making a choice, go with the heart, and even the heaviest of burdens will be worth bearing.

VII · THE CHARIOT — *Keywords: Action, Progress, Energy, Travel, Confidence.* A creaking sound anticipated the arrival of the *katasharin* (片車輪, literally: "single wheel") from the thick night fog. To a woman who peeked out at it, the hag on the chariot said: "Instead of looking at me, have a look at your own child!" When she did, the baby was gone. The woman cursed her negligence and nailed an apologetic letter on her door; when the *katasharin* read it, it decided to return the baby to his mother. This ought to teach you to address things directly instead of prying from the sidelines. Approach your projects, issues, and fears with determination and accept your responsibilities, and you will certainly be rewarded.

VIII · STRENGTH — *Keywords: Fortitude, Endurance, Composure, Patience, Serenity. Kintarō* (金太郎, literally: "golden boy") was a child with superhuman strength, raised by a witch upon Mount Ashigara. His battle against a giant koi fish is a recurring subject in Japanese folklore and tattoo culture, which employs it as a symbol of fortitude and good luck. This Arcanum reminds you that equating strength with mere physical force is a mistake. By taming the fish with calm and composure,

Kintarō shows how attitude can overcome obstacles of any size. True power resides in an indomitable spirit, and a good stance always wins over a simple thrashing around. Strength of character is what you truly need to handle "slippery" situations.

IX · THE HERMIT — *Keywords: Guidance, Meditation, Prudence, Humility, Withdrawal.* As a wandering spirit of the Japanese mountains, the *daitengu* (大天狗, literally: "great divine dog") is closely associated with the ascetic practice of *Shugendō*, the withdrawal from civil society to achieve spiritual realization. This winged *yōkai* wears the same garments of the monks who worship him as a venerable sage of the mountains. Take inspiration to do the same: withdraw into your intimacy and meditate to achieve enlightenment. Look into yourself for guidance and advance with prudence to find the right path across the steep mountain range you are now facing.

X · THE WHEEL — *Keywords: Destiny, Revolution, Repetition, Alternation, Fortune.* Nimble and elusive, the entities known as *kodama* (木霊, literally: "tree spirit") inhabit lush Japanese forests, nesting in tree trunks and hiding within the foliage of the thick canopy. While meeting them is considered a sign of good luck, cutting down one of their homes is an omen of misfortune, and that is why many ancient trees are still protected by *shimenawa* ropes. The moral of this legend is to not interfere with natural cycles. Don't cry over rotting branches, and avoid cutting down healthy roots. Things will change according to their own momentum; accepting and following the flow is the best way to avoid being crushed by the Wheel's never-ending spin.

XI · JUSTICE — *Keywords: Fairness, Balance, Valor, Logic, Insensitivity.* *Zenko* (善狐, literally: "good fox") is the name to describe a benevolent type of *kitsune*, the famous fox-like spirits of Japanese folklore who employ their shapeshifting powers for good. The greater the number of tails, the older and wiser the *zenko*. It is believed that, once the ninth tail is obtained, the *kitsune* becomes able to see and hear anything happening in the world, thus achieving infinite wisdom. Always act with the certainty that an impartial observer watches over you, passing judgment on your actions. The means always come before the ends—that's why acting rightfully, regardless of the outcome, is always a priority.

XII · THE HANGED ONE — *Keywords: Transcendence, Inversion, Perspective, Acceptance, Epiphany.* Often disguised as a young and beautiful lady, the *jorōgumo* (絡新婦, literally: "entangling bride") exposes her true nature once the prey is too close to escape, dragging him into her spidery clasp to devour his essence. Beware of the traps along the path and refrain from charging head-on into situations, because sometimes perils are not easily at sight. Looking at the road ahead from a different angle might reveal the spiderwebs glittering in the sunlight. Sometimes it might even be necessary to reverse your entire perspective in order to find the epiphany you have long been waiting for.

XIII · DEATH — *Keywords: End, Passage, Transformation, Cleansing, Irreversibility.* When the goddess *Izanami* (イザナミ) died, her brother and husband *Izanagi* decided to venture into the underworld to retrieve her. However, frightened by the horrid and rotting body of what once was his beautiful companion, the god fled, chased by the curses and minions of *Izanami*. As he performed ritualistic cleansing, *Izanagi* gave birth to the deities known as the Three Precious Children. This story shows the hardships of loss, but facing and processing the irreversible is the only way to overcome it. Don't let the past torment you. Death is but a passage that leaves place for the new.

XIV · TEMPERANCE — *Keywords: Mediation, Adaptation, Compromise, Harmony, Regeneration.* The mermaid-like creature known as *ningyo* (人魚, literally: "human fish") is thought to populate the waters of Japan since times immemorial. Sights of this *yōkai* fill the stories of the sailors, and the notion that eating its flesh would impart longevity is tied to the legend of Yao Bikuni, an 800-year-old priestess. This elegant creature represents the quality of moderation, of harmony between the parts—human and fish, water and earth. Practice inner balance by mediating your impulses and by carefully blending the opposing forces within you. Feeding off this Arcanum will set off the healing process you need to undergo at this moment.

XV · THE DEVIL — *Keywords: Temptation, Obsession, Selfishness, Indulgence, Taboo.* In Japanese Noh theater plays, the mask of the *hannya* (般若, meaning "Buddha's wisdom") represents the spirit of a woman who has become a demon due to obsession or jealousy. Her face, once beautiful and kind, is long lost behind a cover of sorrow and resentment. This is the destiny of all people eroded by harsh sentiments, so make sure to resist the call of these impulses. Don't be afraid to indulge in your passions, and never refrain from the arts and pleasures that make life worth living, but beware of excesses, for they may consume your identity and tarnish your soul for good.

XVI · THE TOWER — *Keywords: Shock, Ruin, Destruction, Liberation, Chaos. Ashinaga* and *tenaga* (足長 and 手長, literally: "long legs" and "long arms" respectively) are a couple of *yōkai* with unusually stretched limbs. They always work together to catch fish along the seashore: the *ashinaga* stays above water thanks to his legs, while the *tenaga*, who sits on his back, uses his long arms to grab the prey with great reach and precision. It may seem like a perfect strategy, but a simple wave is enough to throw them off balance and lose all the fish caught so far. This ought to teach you how even the best structures can fall due to unforeseen events. The crash might be painful, but the lesson will be crucial to build back a stronger and more efficient system.

XVII · THE STAR — *Keywords: Hope, Clarity, Tranquility, Purity, Direction.* According to the legends, once the gods had finished shaping the animals, all remaining pieces were put together to form a new tapir-like creature: the *baku* (獏). This bizarre *yōkai* feeds on bad dreams and is considered an amulet and a helper that kids can call at night when they need to fend off nightmares. This beast—just like this Arcanum—appears when the time is darkest to shed light upon the road ahead. It is a symbol of hope, the living proof that all spare pieces will fall into the right place at the end. Keep this feeling close to your heart as protection as you pursue the luminous dream that shines in the black of the night.

XVIII · THE MOON — *Keywords: Mystery, Illusion, Subconsciousness, Romanticism, Occultism.* Look at the full moon, and in the dark markings on its surface you will see the shape of a rabbit, working with a mortar and pestle. Ask about it, and the Japanese will tell you of the mythical Moon Hare, pounding ingredients for *Tsukimi*, the Mid-Autumn Festival. The legend of this lunar character is as oneiric and romantic as the moon itself, and equally mysterious. What is the rabbit preparing? Is it food, medicine, or something else? Some things can only be inferred, so use your intuition instead of your rationality to draw your conclusions. The subconscious can be deceiving sometimes, but reason cannot open all doors on its own.

XIX · THE SUN — *Keywords: Truth, Glory, Happiness, Honesty, Exuberance. Amaterasu* (天照, literally: "heaven's light"), goddess of the sun, chief deity of the Shinto pantheon, rules over the heavenly realms with glory and wisdom. According to legend, her descendant became the first emperor of Japan, founding a lineage that persists to this day. The bright rays of *Amaterasu* warm every corner of the world, and bring all secrets to the light of day. It is a time for honesty, growth, and celebration. Invest new energies with enthusiasm; bask in the light of the day, but never stop and stare directly at it, because the sun blinds those who face it with arrogance.

XX · JUDGEMENT — *Keywords: Awakening, Revelation, Redemption, Emergence, Release.* Rejected by the monk she so desperately loved, a young girl named *Kiyohime* (清姫, "princess Kiyo") transformed into a snake and followed him around Japan. The poor man tried to hide inside the bell of a temple, but *Kiyohime* found him and coiled around the iron cage, burning the monk inside it with her fiery breath. This is a wake-up call to remind you that judgment cannot be escaped, no matter how far you can run or how well you can hide. Change is on the way; revelation will bring revolution. Listen for the bell in the distance—it is tolling for you!

XXI · THE WORLD — ***Keywords: Fulfillment, Accomplishment, Integration, Reward, Satisfaction.*** All of Japan lies on the back of the great *Ōnamazu* (大鯰, literally: "giant catfish"), who dwells deep within the Earth. Whenever the guardian-god *Takemikazuchi* gets distracted, *Ōnamazu* thrashes, and earthquakes shake the Land of the Rising Sun. This enormous, legendary beast represents accomplishments of massive stature. A little movement is crucial if you don't want to stagnate in this privileged position, but make sure to have a *Takemikazuchi* around to keep sentiments like arrogance or exuberance at bay, or the world that now lies on your shoulders will crumble down upon you.

CUPS

The Suit of Cups is related to the element of Water. It is a feminine Suit, receptive in nature, and it pertains to the emotional sphere.

The Cup is here represented by the *hyōtan* (瓢箪, "calabash"), the famous bottle gourd used in Japan.

ACE OF CUPS — *Keywords: Emotion, Memory, Care, Openness, Peace.* Good news and prosperity await those who witness the *amabie* (アマビエ), the legendary three-tailed mermaid with a bird-like beak. Her emerging from the depths of the ocean is considered a positive omen, and sketches of her are still used to fend off illness and bad luck. Her appearance in your Spread will bring the same benefits: an outpouring of serenity, joy, nourishment, and abundance into your life.

2 OF CUPS — *Keywords: Attraction, Affinity, Reciprocity, Agreement, Pact.* The *kaijin* (海人, literally: "sea human") are underwater creatures with piscine features. They have a reputation for being ill-tempered and obnoxious, and the fact that even they can come to terms is proof that love can be stronger than any division. This might serve you as a reminder to reunite with a partner, or finally overcome your shyness and express your feeling to your loved one. If a dispute is currently in place, it might be time to put it to rest.

3 OF CUPS — *Keywords: Communion, Frivolity, Dance, Excitement, Intoxication.* When the *ningyo* (人魚, literally: "human fish") come together to celebrate above the surface, then it really must be time to rejoice. These *yōkai* are coy and elusive creatures, so to see three of them dancing is an occasion of rare beauty. Consider this a sign of positive outcomes waiting around the corner, conflict resolution, and good friendship. Enjoy these blissful days—just don't overdo with the celebrations!

4 OF CUPS — *Keywords: Boredom, Apathy, Disenchantment, Distraction, Expectation. Kawauso* (川獺, literally: "river otter") are funny-looking creatures who like to drink, laugh, and play tricks on humans. Some even disguise themselves as beggars just to sneak into the villages and steal some alcohol. If this *kawauso* is refusing sake, it means something must be really off. You might be too distracted to notice an opportunity, or maybe you have just had enough of it all—either way, action is necessary to restore a healthy thirst for life.

5 OF CUPS — *Keywords: Repentance, Loss, Refusal, Despair, Regret.* Just like the more common *kappa*, the *garappa* (ガラッパ) populate the streams and ponds of Japan, where they like to pull pranks on unsuspecting swimmers and sailors. However, all joy seems to have vanished for this solitary *garappa*, who mourns the passing of its cups. Not all hope is lost, of course: two cups are still there, but it is hard to notice the light at the end of the tunnel when you are turning your back on new opportunities. What is missing should not ruin what is still there.

6 OF CUPS — *Keywords: Nostalgia, Longing, Friendship, Altruism, Safety. Amefurikozō* (雨降小僧, literally: "rainfall priest boy") and *ameonna* (雨女, literally: "rain woman") are servants of *Ushi*, the god of rain. Their childlike appearance evokes a deep sense of nostalgia that persists throughout time, following you like drizzle does with these little *yōkai*. The umbrella on the *amefurikozō* is a suggestion to use this feeling as a shelter, a safe and intimate space to rely on when bad weather comes. Make use of this tool and extend it to others, but never bask in the rain for too long, or you will forget the need for a new, sunny day.

7 OF CUPS — *Keywords: Fantasy, Vision, Variety, Selection, Envy.* The black giant *umibōzu* (海坊主, literally: "sea priest") emerges from the ocean and always demands a barrel from the sailors, so he can use it to scoop up water on the deck and sink their ship. The only way to avoid this fate is to give the *umibōzu* a bottomless cask and escape as it foolishly attempts to fill it up. As you can see, selection is fundamental to achieve your goals, so evaluate all options carefully. Dream big, but temper your wishes—a bottomless appetite will bog you down.

8 OF CUPS — *Keywords: Release, Waiver, Shyness, Farsightedness, Adventure.* When a turban snail reaches 30 years of age, it may transform into the creature known as *sazae-oni* (栄螺鬼, literally: "turban shell demon"). The dance of this mollusk demon below the night sky to celebrate the long-awaited transition is an exhortation to abandon your comfort zone and search for more. The journey may be long, hard, or lonely, but winning over fears and shyness is the only way to emerge from your hide-out to finally explore the land.

9 OF CUPS — *Keywords: Contentment, Pleasure, Virtue, Sensuality, Saturation.* The *kawaguma* (川熊, literally: "river bear") is a feral *yōkai* that lives at the bottom of deep rivers, away from human eyes, and is said to collect the objects that fall from ferryboats and bridges. Of course, this creature communicates a sense of profound satisfaction, but the wealth accumulated can prove damaging in the long run. You might need to let go of some ballast to emerge and see the sunlight again.

10 OF CUPS — *Keywords: Success, Conclusion, Recognition, Family, Rest.* A family of *fuchizaru* (淵猿, literally: "abyss monkey") rest happily before a waterfall. Rain has just come to an end, and a beautiful rainbow glistens in the sunlight. This is an encouraging omen, a sign that a troublesome situation is coming to a happy end. The positive resolution arrives with gifts from the heavens to you and those you hold dearest, be they friends, family, or lovers. Enjoy these moments.

PAGE OF CUPS — *Keywords: Receptivity, Sweetness, Kindness, Perception, Grace. Nure-onna* (濡女, literally: "wet woman") is a reptilian *yōkai* with the looks of a beautiful girl. According to legends, it usually appears along the seashores with a baby in her hands, asking travelers to hold it for a moment. If the traveler tries to leave it when the creature is gone, the bundle becomes heavy, blocking the holder for the *nure-onna* to come back and devour him. This cautionary tale is not just about caring for a baby: it is a metaphor to show how qualities like kindness and grace can benefit you, regardless of the person they are directed to.

KNIGHT OF CUPS — *Keywords: Seduction, Flattery, Encouragement, Temperament, Warm. Ichimoku nyudo* (一目入道, literally: "one-eyed priest") is the guardian of Lake Kamo, on the island of Sado, in Niigata Prefecture. This water creature is said to resurface once every year to wander on land, driven by curiosity and revenge toward the human that once stole its magic fish hook. It represents advancement and attitude, but also the allure of mysterious and forbidden places. Pursue with courage the path set by your heart.

KING OF CUPS — *Keywords: Loyalty, Composure, Calm, Affection, Sympathy.* The Sea of Japan hides great and powerful creatures, and one of these is the *oshōuo* (和尚魚, literally: "high priest fish"). This turtle-bodied *yōkai* with a monk's head is calm and placid: if it gets caught in a sailor's nets, it will simply ask the man to free it. If the human refuses, however, he will incur a terrible curse. It is important to approach everyone with a composed and helping attitude, but it is just as crucial to respond adequately to abuse.

QUEEN OF CUPS — *Keywords: Sensitivity, Tolerance, Forgiveness, Tenderness, Support. Kawahime* (川姫, literally: "river princess") is a spirit of the streams who lives underneath bridges or near watermills along the riversides. There she waits for travelers to come by, attracting them with her beauty only to drain their vital energy. To avoid this fate, one must lower his head, avoid eye contact, and carry on. Similarly, life might sometimes urge you to tolerate, forgive, and even forget a person or a situation in order to pass by without getting hurt.

COINS

The Suit of Coins is related to the element of Earth. It is a feminine Suit, receptive in nature, and it pertains to the material sphere.

The Coin is here represented by the *mon* and *koban* (文 and 小判, respectively), the round and oval coins used in Japan until the late nineteenth century.

ACE OF COINS — *Keywords: Gain, Fortune, Materialism, Possession, Start.* The body of a deer, the scales of a dragon, the tail of an ox, and a glowing, golden mane—the *kirin* (麒麟) is one of the rarest, noblest, and most beautiful creatures in all of East Asia. It is a beast of pure goodness, and its hooves do not trample any insect or blade of grass, so as to not lose a single living thing. This means gain and prosperity are the only things on the horizon, because fortune and peace will bless the lucky witness of the holy *kirin.*

2 OF COINS — *Keywords: Duality, Gaiety, Flexibility, Juggle, Inconstancy. Yamaotoko* (山男, literally: "mountain man") is a rugged but gentle giant who lives hidden in the Japanese forests. He appears in the famous story of a man who had to rush down the mountains to call a doctor for an ill relative: such was the hurry that he slipped and broke his leg, but was later rescued by *yamaotoko*. Both the man and his friend's lives were saved in the end, but beware: if you can't handle multiple things at once, quit before you hurt yourself.

3 OF COINS — *Keywords: Craft, Art, Project, Talent, Inspiration.* The origin of the *ippondatara* (一本踏鞴, literally: "one-legged bellows") is shrouded in mystery. Some say it used to be a woodsman who had to cut off one of his legs in penance for a crime. Others claim it was actually a blacksmith, who lost an eye after staring at the intense flames of the furnace for too long. Either way, it is a tale of craft and dedication to the arts. Pursue your projects with passion, but plan them out carefully, unless you want to end up scarred like the *ippondatara*.

4 OF COINS — *Keywords: Greed, Thrift, Control, Inheritance, Investment. Sarugami* (猿神, literally: "monkey god") are ape-like creatures that populate the mountains of Japan. Once revered as spirits dear to the sun, they gradually lost ground to the expanding civilization and are now confined to the forests, from which they raid villages to steal crops, food, money, and even children. Their stance to protect their home is inspiring, but their possessive behavior and avarice are attitudes you must definitely stay away from.

5 OF COINS — *Keywords: Need, Poverty, Struggle, Obstacle, Cold.* The *binbōgami* (貧乏神, literally: "god of poverty") is a spirit that brings misery and struggle to the house it is haunting. According to the stories, if the *binbōgami* is shown hospitality and respect, then it will leave the home and bless it with a streak of good fortune. The appearance of this *yōkai* foreshadows hard times, but proves that virtues like generosity and kindness in moments of difficulty can get you back up on your feet, and even stronger than before.

6 OF COINS — *Keywords: Generosity, Charity, Distribution, Empathy, Offer.* To save its kin from further killings, a silver *kitsune* (狐, literally: "fox") once disguised itself as a famous monk named Hakuzōsu and bought all the snares from a cruel trapper. It had to maintain this shape for over fifty years to ensure the safety of the foxes,

and when death finally exposed it, even humans built a shrine in its honor. As you can see, even though altruism requires sacrifice, the rewards and the glory are much greater.

7 OF COINS — *Keywords: Evaluation, Expansion, Duty, Development, Patience.* *Ta-no-kami* (田の神, literally: "god of the rice paddies") is the spirit that watches over the harvest. It is invoked to bring good fruits in the next season, but its relevance spans over the mere agricultural scope: it is a symbol of patience and pacing. Most importantly, it proves something that may sound counterintuitive to most: the idea that waiting can be the most productive act there is. Apply this concept and allow your situations to bloom.

8 OF COINS — *Keywords: Work, Habit, Commitment, Autonomy, Finesse.* In the accounts of the legendary warrior Minamoto no Yorimitsu appears an ominous creature known as *tsuchigumo* (土蜘蛛, literally: "earth spider"). This giant, shapeshifting arachnid always devises cunning strategies to trick and devour Yorimitsu, but never succeeds. Despite the cruel nature of the *yōkai*, its titanic dedication to an impossible goal is a quality to admire. Apply yourself and refine your craft as the *tsuchigumo* does with his plans and spiderwebs.

9 OF COINS — *Keywords: Prudence, Independence, Education, Assurance, Richness.* One of many different versions of the origin of *futakuchi-onna* (二口女, literally: "two-mouthed woman") involves a miser who never let his wife eat. This led to the opening of a second mouth on the woman's nape, which started to feed itself using the hair as hands to bring food to its gnarling jaws. This is a story of emancipation and independence. Problematic situations will resolve as you develop secondary skills to take better care of them.

10 OF COINS — *Keywords: Wealth, Legacy, Link, Culmination, Home.* The strange *bake ichō no sei* (化け銀杏の精, literally: "changed ginkgo spirit") is said to appear near old ginkgo trees to strike its mallet on a gong and make itself heard. The ginkgo tree, a species that first appeared over 290 million years ago, is a symbol of the resilience that this *yōkai* brings attention to. The sound of its gong reminds you of the importance of heritage and tradition, and announces the passing on of physical as well as immaterial wealth.

PAGE OF COINS — *Keywords: Effort, Study, Practicality, Curiosity, Examination.* A strange curse is said to affect certain women at night, making their neck stretch and their heads roam around freely. These *yōkai* are called *rokurokubi* (ろくろ首, literally: "pulley neck"), and they are a popular appearance among Japanese folk tales. This spirit can be seen as a representation of unbridled curiosity—after all, a wandering head is a wondering mind. It is a positive thing, of course—just make sure not to get carried away by curiosity or stretch yourself too thin with study.

KNIGHT OF COINS — *Keywords: Adaptability, Pragmatism, Persistency, Professionalism, Dependability.* On a giant toad stands a *kinoko* (木の子, literally: "child of the tree"), a boy-like spirit of the forest, usually dressed in leaves and branches. This *yōkai* is a common encounter for Japanese woodcutters, who often see their lunch boxes stolen by this mischievous spirit at the first moment of distraction. The presence of a *kinoko* requires you to focus and carry on your task with diligence—unless you want to see everything acquired so far disappear in the blink of an eye.

KING OF COINS — *Keywords: Business, Enterprise, Money, Administration, Maturation.* The undisputed king of Japanese forests is the mighty *Inozasaō* (猪笹王 literally: "boar bamboo king"), a wild, hog-like creature with leaves and vines growing on its back. Its presence protects the nature around Nara, and its shapeshifting powers give life to encounters that are now part of the local folklore. Take inspiration from *Inozasaō*'s authority and responsibility in pursuing your enterprises, and soon you too will bear the succulent fruits of success.

QUEEN OF COINS — *Keywords: Conservation, Conscience, Nurture, Heart, Discretion.* The *yamahime* (山姫, literally: "mountain princess") are female spirits who live deep in the woods of Japanese mountains. Usually, they are solitary and quiet, but can become aggressive and brutal with those who invade their spaces or disrespect the vegetation or animals of the forest. Sometimes harsh measures are necessary to preserve what is important. Take special care of things and people dear to you.

WANDS

The Suit of Wands is related to the element of Fire. It is a masculine Suit, assertive in nature, and it pertains to the passional sphere.

The Wand is here represented by the *shakujō* (錫杖, literally: "tin cane"), a ceremonial staff topped with iron rings, used by monks to chant and shoo away the animals encountered during their peregrination.

ACE OF WANDS — *Keywords: Creativity, Originality, Adventure, Strength, Spark.* Tales of a strange floating fire in the Shiga and Kyoto Prefectures gave rise to the legend of the *abura-bō* (油坊, literally: "oil priest"), a wandering fire spirit born out of the soul of a monk who had stolen oil from a lamp. It is a story of thievery and impulse, a sudden burst of initiative that changes life for good. Be it positive or negative, this is the spark that sets off a new adventure, the sacred flame that reveals a new path, fueled by the oil of creation.

2 OF WANDS — *Keywords: Plan, Aspiration, Drive, Restlessness, Arrogance. Gotoku neko* (五徳猫, literally: "cat of the five virtues") is a two-tailed *yōkai* that hangs around fires and stokes the flames by blowing through pipes of bamboo. This gesture has the power to revive hidden embers below the ashes, preparing a new fire to cook the upcoming course. Your projects will benefit from this careful preparation, just make sure to not blow too eagerly on the flame—arrogance always backfires.

3 OF WANDS — *Keywords: Anticipation, Observation, Attention, Delay, Foresight.* Toward the end of the tenth century, several monks burned themselves alive in ritual fire to get rid of their worldly attachments and achieve enlightenment. Those who could not fully give up the material realm are now called *kazenbō* (火前坊, literally: "monk before the flames") and are cursed to haunt the place of their death. They serve as a reminder of the damage eagerness can do in the pursuit of a goal. Things are in motion; wait for the best time to act.

4 OF WANDS — *Keywords: Celebration, Preparation, Tranquility, Perfectionism, Solidity.* At night, chains of hundreds or thousands of floating lights might appear in the most secluded places. As lanterns carried by invisible bearers, these lights dance in a sacred procession. They are called *kitsunebi*

(狐火, literally: "fox fires"), and they signal a *yōkai* parade, wedding, or meeting. Their appearance foretells the arrival of a joyous occasion, a time to rejoice with friends and family, or simply a gathering to ensure stability.

5 OF WANDS — *Keywords: Competition, Rivalry, Conflict, Training, Imitation.* The islands of Okinawa are home to many unique *yōkai*, and one of these is the extravagant *kijimunā* (キジムナー), a little elf-like creature that dwells on banyan trees. *Kijimunā* are particularly spiteful and belligerent; they play tricks on humans and have very peculiar prejudices against cooking pots, octopuses, and chickens. Their competitive behavior is certainly a feature to be inspired by, but make sure to know what is worth fighting for.

6 OF WANDS — *Keywords: Victory, Fame, Vanity, Diplomacy, News.* For one night each year, a parade of one hundred *oni* and *yōkai* fills the streets of many towns in Japan. A one-eyed spirit known as *Yagyō San* (夜行さん, literally: "the man of the night parade") leads the procession on his headless horse, trampling any mortal who dares to interrupt. Apply the same principle in your successes: celebrate the triumph, and don't let anyone spoil the celebration—just avoid being excessively zealous.

7 OF WANDS — *Keywords: Defense, Opposition, Opinion, Battle, Nonconformity.* A popular group activity of the Edo period consisted of lighting up a hundred lanterns and telling each other progressively scarier ghost stories. After each story, one lantern would be snuffed out. At the hundredth tale, a dark spirit was said to appear from the darkness to scare and attack the guests: the *aoandon* (青行燈, literally: "blue lantern"). This *yōkai* is an omen of battle. Feel free to make your voice heard, but get ready to back up your words.

8 OF WANDS — *Keywords: Speed, Movement, Swiftness, Reaction, Expedition.* Pale blue lights often appear in the Japanese countryside, hovering softly above ground and water as orbs of burning air. These mysterious flames are called *onibi* (鬼火, literally: "demon fire"), and they are said to be the souls of humans and animals who cannot go on to the afterlife. The *onibi* is an example of the pain produced by lingering, of the sadness created by stagnation. Be inspired by this to pursue your endeavors with energy and swiftness.

9 OF WANDS — *Keywords: Guard, Vigilance, Tenacity, Threshold, Experience.* The legend of the *abura-akago* (油赤子, literally: "oil red baby") tells of a spirit intruding in homes at night, disguised as a baby to lick all the oil out of the lanterns. Despite mentioning a theft, this story bears much larger implications about thresholds and their protection. It foreshadows a threat to your personal space, which you need to guard attentively. Beware, because menaces often come in deceivingly harmless shapes.

10 OF WANDS — *Keywords: Fatigue, Toil, Oppression, Burnout, Completion.* A terrible, flaming feline spirit, the *kasha* (火車, literally: "fire cart") appears during funeral services, leaping down from rooftops to snatch bodies out of their coffins in order to eat them or use them as puppets. Because of them, priests started celebrating a fake burial to bait the *kasha* before the official ceremony. This story literally mentions a "dead weight" you should let off your shoulders. Stop running: the time to rest has come.

PAGE OF WANDS — *Keywords: Initiative, Vitality, Excitement, Playfulness, Risk.*

Deep in the bamboo groves of the island of Shikoku hides the fire bird called *basan* (波山, from the sound of its flapping wings). This legendary beast breathes ghost-fire, a cold flame that does not burn or light up, and is told to disappear as soon as it is sighted. This *yōkai* represents a young and playful soul looking for adventure. Be careful, though: that fire is unripe, and a sterile defense against the perils you may find along the way.

KNIGHT OF WANDS — *Keywords: Courage, Momentum, Distance, Idealism, Recklessness.* A *bake-danuki* (化け狸, literally: "changed raccoon") rides on the back of a wild boar. Its body is cloaked by a blue flame, but the *yōkai* shows no fear—its gaze is calm, and its expression determined. This scene represents sheer drive, the willingness to go through fire in order to achieve your goals. If the object of your desire is out of reach, don't be afraid to ask for the help necessary to speed up the process. Don't let your wish run away.

KING OF WANDS — *Keywords: Leadership, Motivation, Persuasion, Wit, Presumption.* A long time ago, at the temple of Mibu-dera, there lived a wicked monk named Sōgen who stole money from the offering box and oil from the lamps. When he died, he was damned to wander around under the guise of a floating, flaming head known as *Sōgen-bi* (叢原火, literally: "Sogen's fire"). This ominous *yōkai* is "living" proof of the risks presumption and haughtiness can subject you to. Accept your responsibilities—after all, that's what a true leader does.

QUEEN OF WANDS — *Keywords: Charisma, Magnetism, Sensuality, Optimism, Vivacity.* The spirit known as *nekomusume* (猫娘, literally: "cat girl") is a recurring *yōkai* in Japanese folk tales. This feline woman with an aristocratic bearing is here accompanied by a *nekomata* (猫又, literally: "forked cat"), a split-tailed beast famous for being particularly malicious and short-tempered. These two figures represent a combination of delicate and aggressive features—the pillars of a charismatic and multifaceted personality you must embody.

SWORDS

The Suit of Swords is related to the element of Air. It is a masculine Suit, assertive in nature, and it pertains to the intellectual sphere.

The Sword is here represented by the *katana* (刀), the world-famous Japanese weapon carried by the samurai warrior class.

ACE OF SWORDS — *Keywords: Thought, Idea, Objectivity, Responsibility, Conviction.* The *Obon* festival is a moment to honor the deceased with rice and sake. The morning after, the spirits of the ancestors travel with a breeze called *shōrōkaze* (精霊風, literally; "ghost wind") to caress those who honored them and scold those who did not. This arcane wind rises suddenly, like an epiphany: use the wings of inspiration to ride it, and fly over problems with the power of new ideas. Beware, however, as it may also bring thoughts of strict discipline and responsibility.

2 OF SWORDS — *Keywords: Duel, Discussion, Duality, Stalemate, Blindness.* The soothing voice of a woman attracts the attention of travelers. Those who decide to answer the call gasp at the sight of the pitch-black smile she displays as she cackles sinisterly. This is *ohaguro-bettari* (お歯黒べったり, literally: "nothing but black teeth"), and she is here to test your decision-making skills. Choose your path and enemies wisely, and beware of excessively enticing options, for their appearance might conceal incredible dangers.

3 OF SWORDS — *Keywords: Sorrow, Pain, Despair, Guilt, Regret.* The *gashadokuro* (がしゃどくろ, from the sound of its chattering teeth) is a giant skeleton spirit born out of the bones of those who died violently on the battlefield. This frightful *yōkai* hunts at night, devouring men until its pent-up anger is finally extinguished. This apparition represents a hurtful event knocking at your door, or a past grudge outliving its cause. Don't give in to despair; face the issue—only then will it turn back into dust.

4 OF SWORDS — *Keywords: Recovery, Sleep, Truce, Retreat, Pause.* In the dark, dusty halls of long-abandoned mansions, one can stumble upon a *yōkai* called *aonyōbo* (青女房, literally: "blue spouse"). This is the spirit of a frustrated courtier, waiting for a lover or a husband who will never return, and devouring any trespasser who disturbs her wait. This cruel spirit is a warning not to obsess over goals and ambitions, because stability of the mind is of the utmost importance. Take time to rest, reflect, and recuperate.

5 OF SWORDS — *Keywords: Selfishness, Complacency, Domination, Revenge, Drama.* During his eastward expedition, the legendary first emperor of Japan was guided by a three-legged crow known as *Yatagarasu* (八咫烏, literally: "eight-span crow"). Thanks to this *yōkai*, the emperor's party managed to traverse the mountains and proceed to establish the country. The coming of *Yatagarasu* urges you to abandon selfishness and excessive pride and power. Be humble and accept outside help if needed, and your kingdom will finally see the light.

6 OF SWORDS — *Keywords: Journey, Escape, Renunciation, Expedience, Transfer.* Lingering between this world and the next, the *yūrei* (幽霊, literally: "faint spirit") represent a close parallel to traditional Western ghosts. Kept out of the afterlife by the unfair conditions of their deaths, these spirits travel to finally reach the final rest.

You too might be on a journey right now, caught between the start and the destination. Feeling adrift is normal when you are in the midst of a search, but new shores will soon be in sight.

7 OF SWORDS — *Keywords: Stealth, Subterfuge, Shortcut, Espionage, Collection.* The *kamaitachi* (鎌鼬, literally: "sickle weasel") rides the swirling whirlwinds of the mountain regions and cuts unfortunate travelers with its sharp claws and spiky fur. Its movement is said to be so fast and stealthy as to be invisible to the naked eye. The *kamaitachi* symbolizes a silent menace, someone lying or plotting behind your back. Alternatively, it may be an invitation for you to be particularly sneaky in approaching the current issue.

8 OF SWORDS — *Keywords: Limit, Lethargy, Paralysis, Trap, Impediment.* The name *ubume* (産女, literally: "birthing woman") describes the ghost of a mother who has passed away during childbirth. With a baby in her arms, this spirit wanders in search of someone to take care of it. Anyone who accepts the bundle can feel it grow heavier and heavier, until it becomes impossible to move. This apparition speaks

of a situation of stasis, possibly brought by a past trauma. Sharing the load might be the right way to overcome the block.

9 OF SWORDS — *Keywords: Anguish, Desperation, Uncertainty, Obscurity, Doubt.* The *nikusui* (肉吸い, literally: "meat sucker") are vampiric *yōkai*, notorious for taking advantage of their beauty to attract victims and then suck the flesh out of them, leaving only skin and bones behind. Yet, this time it is the "monster" itself who wakes up from a terrible nightmare. This might be the result of sudden doubts, guilt, or pain for an obsessive behavior. Confront the issue openly to strip it of its daunting and fearful charge.

10 OF SWORDS — *Keywords: Affliction, Block, Desolation, Fear, Finish.* Pierced by the blades of ten sharp *katana*, a woman lies dead on the ground. When the mortal body is lost, the soul persists as a *yūrei* (幽霊, literally: "faint spirit"), which parts from the body once and for all. This scene ought to teach you not to cling to remnants of a past that will never come back. Accepting defeat is the only way forward, but do not despair, because a loss is but the prelude of transcendence.

PAGE OF SWORDS — *Keywords: Eagerness, Cleverness, Genius, Calculation, Help.* Secluded upon the peaks they love and protect, the *daitengu* (大天狗, literally: "great divine dog") are winged creatures with a red face and a long nose. The monks of the mountains admire and respect the cunning of these creatures—and so should you. Be vigilant and protect what you love dearly with the same cleverness of a *daitengu*, but remember to look beyond your lonely peak if you want to learn more and better yourself.

KNIGHT OF SWORDS — *Keywords: Dexterity, Impatience, Valor, Haste, Frankness.* If a set of tiny footprints mysteriously appears in your home, follow it: it might lead you to a *zashiki warashi* (座敷童子, literally: "parlor child"). It is said that those who withstand its juvenile pranks may obtain good fortune, while those who lose their temper and shoo it away will receive trouble. This ought to remind you to reflect before acting and to make honorable decisions. Being smart and impatient makes you jump to conclusions at times.

KING OF SWORDS — *Keywords: Rationality, Analysis, Precision, Tactic, Focus.*

Fūjin (風神, literally: "wind god") is the divinity that governs the air. His cloth bag safeguards the winds of the world, which he sometimes lets loose in order to fight his brother *Raijin*, the god of lightning, thunder, and storms. This godly figure is here to inspire you: affirm yourself and devise cunning plans to take control of the current situation. If fighting someone close to you is the only logical solution to the problem, don't hesitate to do so.

QUEEN OF SWORDS — *Keywords: Straightforwardness, Strategy, Rigor, Concision, Discipline.* The *kaze no kami* (風の神, literally: "spirits of the wind") are *yōkai* of the air realm, traveling with the gusts across Japan to bring their influence to bear upon humanity. Their breath can be either positive and fresh or negative and pestilent, depending on their intentions. Similarly to this *kaze no kami*, your actions must be swift and direct. Open your mouth only to benefit the worthy or punish the undeserving, with no in-between.

YŌKAI TAROT

INTRODUZIONE

Chi ha poca familiarità con gli *yōkai* tende a identificarli come un banale insieme di mostri esotici e fantasmi, ma nulla potrebbe essere più lontano dalla verità. Difatti, queste creature rappresentano una parte integrante del patrimonio culturale giapponese e derivano direttamente dalla sua religione indigena, lo shintoismo, che sostiene la tesi animistica secondo cui gli enti naturali – e persino alcuni oggetti – sarebbero dotati di anima e intelletto. Questa convinzione dà vita a un mondo magico permeato di senzienza e significato, dove ogni cosa possiede una volontà propria con cui è possibile interagire.

In poche parole, gli *yōkai* rappresentano la personificazione di tutti i fenomeni della realtà e, dunque, trattare con loro significa trattare con la realtà stessa.

Vista in quest'ottica, la combinazione con uno strumento di indagine come quello dei Tarocchi appare quanto mai ovvia e naturale, poiché definisce il punto d'incontro tra due meccanismi perfettamente complementari: la manifestazione del mondo come interlocutore immanente e il potere comunicativo dei 78 Arcani per avviare un dialogo che aiuti a comprenderlo e affrontarlo.

Ecco, lo Yōkai Tarot è proprio il frutto di questa speciale combinazione.

STESA DEL TORII

Questa Stesa, progettata specificamente per lo Yōkai Tarot, ha la forma di un *torii*, i famosi portali ubicati all'ingresso dei santuari shintoisti. Il *torii* rappresenta una soglia tra il regno terreno e quello spirituale e, in quanto tale, introduce il lettore a livelli di coscienza più elevati. Questa Stesa deve essere usata specificamente come guida alla meditazione: costruisci il tuo *torii* pezzo dopo pezzo, riflettendo sui vari livelli, per poi attraversarlo e raggiungere l'illuminazione.

1-2: I principi alla base del viaggio; i valori che devono guidare ogni tuo passo. Queste fondamenta supporteranno il peso della costruzione che sta per sorgere, fungendo da pilastri concettuali per la nuova struttura.

3-4: Ciò che devi lasciare andare per procedere; episodi, persone o idee che puoi ora "assestare" sulla solidità dei pilastri appena eretti. Quelli che una volta erano considerati fardelli devono essere superati e trasformati in blocchi di esperienza su cui continuare a costruire. Il rilascio ti rende leggero e libero di ascendere.

5-6: L'epifania alla fine del viaggio; il punto di svolta della tua coscienza. I nuovi valori ti hanno permesso di abbandonare le questioni terrene e, nel rilasciarle, queste si sono trasformate in lezioni preziose. Ora la tua mente è pronta a librarsi tra le verità celesti per completare la sua evoluzione.

ARCANI MAGGIORI

0 · IL MATTO — *Parole chiave: Libertà, Spontaneità, Innocenza, Follia, Ingenuità.* Camminare a testa alta permette di avere una buona visuale sull'orizzonte, ma impedisce di notare ciò che si trova sotto i piedi. L'avventura è sia liberatoria che pericolosa: goditela con cautela!

I · IL BAGATTO — *Parole chiave: Volontà, Abilità, Ambizione, Inganno, Menzogna.* Dedicati ai tuoi progetti e affina i tuoi numerosi talenti, ma poi assicurati di prendere una direzione definitiva e non girare a vuoto.

II · LA PAPESSA — *Parole chiave: Saggezza, Intuizione, Segretezza, Introspezione, Severità.* Confida nella certezza che forze più grandi di te sono all'opera per indirizzare il tuo cammino. Aguzza l'intuito per individuare i segnali più criptici e confusi.

III · L'IMPERATRICE — *Parole chiave: Abbondanza, Fertilità, Eleganza, Bellezza, Protezione.* Amore e appartenenza sono le qualità da incarnare: esse condurranno a ricchezza e fecondità, ma anche alla nobiltà d'animo necessaria per mettere tutto a beneficio degli altri.

IV · L'IMPERATORE — *Parole chiave: Potere, Autorità, Disciplina, Esperienza, Precisione.* Prendi in mano la situazione e controllala; stabilisci dei confini e difendili. Tuttavia, assicurati di essere rispettato piuttosto che temuto: severità e crudeltà sono due cose ben diverse.

V · IL PAPA — *Parole chiave: Conoscenza, Ispirazione, Fede, Conformità, Gerarchia.* Analizza a fondo la situazione, perché potrebbe esserci più di quel che sembra. Segui pure le tradizioni e integrati nella società, ma non snaturarti del tutto nel farlo.

VI · GLI AMANTI — *Parole chiave: Gioia, Passione, Unione, Desiderio, Scelta.* Talvolta sono necessari sacrifici per stabilire un legame significativo. Se una scelta è fatta col cuore, anche il fardello più pesante varrà la pena di essere portato.

VII · IL CARRO — *Parole chiave: Azione, Progresso, Energia, Viaggio, Fiducia.* Affronta le cose direttamente. Approccia i progetti, i problemi e le paure con determinazione e accetta le tue responsabilità: sarai sicuramente ricompensato.

VIII · LA FORZA — *Parole chiave: Coraggio, Resistenza, Compostezza, Pazienza, Serenità.* La vera forza risiede in uno spirito indomito; una buona postura vince sempre sul semplice dimenarsi. Il carattere è ciò che serve davvero per gestire situazioni "scivolose".

IX · L'EREMITA — *Parole chiave: Guida, Meditazione, Prudenza, Umiltà, Ritiro.* Ritirati nella tua intimità per meditare e raggiungere l'illuminazione; cerca dentro di te la guida che cerchi e avanza con prudenza per trovare un passo tra le montagne.

X · LA RUOTA — *Parole chiave: Destino, Rivoluzione, Ripetizione, Alternanza, Fortuna.* Non interferire coi cicli naturali: le cose cambiano secondo il proprio ritmo, e accettare e seguire il flusso è il modo migliore per evitare di essere schiacciati dall'infinito girare della Ruota.

XI · LA GIUSTIZIA — *Parole chiave: Equità, Equilibrio, Valore, Logica, Insensi-*

bilità. Agisci sempre come se un osservatore imparziale vegliasse su di te, vagliando le tue azioni. La correttezza è sempre una priorità, indipendentemente dai risultati.

XII · L'APPESO — *Parole chiave: Trascendenza, Inversione, Prospettiva, Accettazione, Epifania.* Fai attenzione alle trappole lungo il cammino e non lanciarti a capofitto nelle situazioni. Potrebbe essere necessario rovesciare la prospettiva attuale per giungere alla soluzione.

XIII · LA MORTE — *Parole chiave: Fine, Passaggio, Trasformazione, Pulizia, Irreversibilità.* Affrontare ed elaborare l'irreversibile è l'unico modo per superarlo. Non lasciare che il passato ti tormenti: la fine è solo il passaggio a un nuovo inizio.

XIV · LA TEMPERANZA — *Parole chiave: Mediazione, Adattamento, Compromesso, Armonia, Rigenerazione.* Pratica l'equilibrio interiore mediando gli impulsi e mescolando con cura le forze opposte dentro di te. La miscela darà il via al processo di guarigione di cui hai bisogno adesso.

XV · IL DIAVOLO — *Parole chiave: Tentazione, Ossessione, Egoismo, Indulgenza, Tabù.* Non avere paura di assecondare le tue passioni e non astenerti mai dai piaceri della vita. Guardati dagli eccessi, piuttosto, poiché rischiano di rovinare il godimento stesso.

XVI · LA TORRE — *Parole chiave: Shock, Rovina, Distruzione, Liberazione, Caos.* Anche le strutture migliori possono cadere a causa di eventi imprevisti. Il crollo è doloroso, ma la lezione sarà fondamentale per ricostruire un sistema più forte ed efficiente.

XVII · LA STELLA — *Parole chiave: Speranza, Chiarezza, Tranquillità, Purezza, Direzione.* Abbi fede: tutti i pezzi cadranno al giusto posto. Tieni questo sentimento vicino al cuore come protezione, mentre insegui il sogno luminoso che brilla nel nero della notte.

XVIII · LA LUNA — *Parole chiave: Mistero, Illusione, Subconscio, Romanticismo, Occultismo.* È il momento di usare l'intuito invece della semplice razionalità. Il subconscio a volte può ingannare, ma la ragione non può aprire tutte le porte da sola.

XIX · IL SOLE — *Parole chiave: Verità, Gloria, Felicità, Onestà, Esuberanza.* Investi nuove energie con entusiasmo. Crogiolati nella luce del sole, ma non fermarti mai a fissarlo direttamente, poiché esso accieca chi lo affronta con arroganza.

XX · IL GIUDIZIO — *Parole chiave: Risveglio, Rivelazione, Redenzione, Emersione, Liberazione.* Non importa quanto lontano si corra o quanto bene ci si possa nascondere: non si può sfuggire al giudizio. Il cambiamento è in arrivo; la rivelazione porterà la rivoluzione.

XXI · IL MONDO — *Parole chiave: Appagamento, Realizzazione, Integrazione, Ricompensa, Soddisfazione.* Un po' di movimento è fondamentale per non stagnare in una posizione privilegiata, ma tieni a bada arroganza ed esuberanza, o il mondo che ora poggia sulle tue spalle ti crollerà addosso.

COPPE

ASSO DI COPPE — *Parole chiave: Emozione, Memoria, Cura, Apertura, Pace.* Un presagio positivo scongiura malattie e sfortuna. C'è un'esplosione di serenità, gioia, nutrimento e abbondanza nella tua vita.

2 DI COPPE — *Parole chiave: Attrazione, Affinità, Reciprocità, Accordo, Patto.* Ricongiungiti con il partner o supera finalmente la timidezza per esprimere i tuoi sentimenti alla persona amata. Se è in corso una disputa, potrebbe essere il momento di risolverla.

3 DI COPPE — *Parole chiave: Comunione, Frivolezza, Danza, Eccitazione, Intossicazione.* I risultati positivi sono dietro l'angolo: è il momento di terminare i conflitti e stabilire nuove amicizie. Goditi questi giorni felici, ma non esagerare con i festeggiamenti!

4 DI COPPE — *Parole chiave: Noia, Apatia, Disincanto, Distrazione, Aspettativa.* Qualcosa non va. Potresti essere troppo distratto per notare un'opportunità, o forse ti sei semplicemente stufato. È necessario agire per ripristinare una sana sete di vita.

5 DI COPPE — *Parole chiave: Pentimento, Perdita, Rifiuto, Disperazione, Rimpianto.* Non tutte le speranze sono perdute, ma è difficile notare la luce alla fine del tunnel quando si voltano le spalle a nuove opportunità. Ciò che manca non deve rovinare ciò che c'è ancora.

6 DI COPPE — *Parole chiave: Nostalgia, Mancanza, Amicizia, Altruismo, Sicurezza.* Trova un riparo, uno spazio sicuro e intimo in cui rifugiarti quando arriva il maltempo. Utilizza questa protezione ed estendila ad altri nell'attesa di una nuova giornata di sole.

7 DI COPPE — *Parole chiave: Fantasia, Visione, Varietà, Selezione, Invidia.* La selezione è un aspetto fondamentale, quindi valuta attentamente tutte le opzioni. Sogna, ma con umiltà: un appetito senza fondo ti può fare impantanare.

8 DI COPPE — *Parole chiave: Liberazione, Rinuncia, Timidezza, Lungimiranza, Avventura.* Abbandona la comfort zone. Il

viaggio può essere lungo, difficile o solitario, ma vincere le paure e la timidezza è l'unico modo per scoprire novità meravigliose.

9 DI COPPE — *Parole chiave: Appagamento, Piacere, Virtù, Sensualità, Saturazione.* La soddisfazione è grande, ma a lungo andare la ricchezza accumulata può rivelarsi dannosa. Potrebbe essere necessario lasciare un po' di zavorra per riemergere e respirare.

10 DI COPPE — *Parole chiave: Successo, Conclusione, Riconoscimento, Famiglia, Riposo.* Una situazione problematica sta per risolversi, e l'esito positivo arriva con dei doni per te e per le persone a te più care. Goditi questi momenti.

FANTE DI COPPE — *Parole chiave: Ricettività, Dolcezza, Gentilezza, Percezione, Grazia.* Qualità come la gentilezza e la grazia possono sempre tornare utili, indipendentemente dai meriti della persona a cui sono rivolte.

CAVALIERE DI COPPE — *Parole chiave: Seduzione, Adulazione, Incoraggiamento, Temperamento, Calore.* Procedi senza timore verso luoghi affascinanti, misteriosi e proibiti. Persegui con coraggio la strada tracciata dal cuore.

RE DI COPPE — *Parole chiave: Lealtà, Compostezza, Calma, Affetto, Simpatia.* È importante approcciare gli altri con atteggiamento amichevole, ma è altrettanto fondamentale rispondere adeguatamente agli abusi.

REGINA DI COPPE — *Parole chiave: Sensibilità, Tolleranza, Perdono, Tenerezza, Sostegno.* Abbassa la testa, evita il contatto visivo e prosegui. A volte occorre tollerare, perdonare e persino dimenticare una persona o una situazione per evitare di essere feriti.

DENARI

ASSO DI DENARI — *Parole chiave: Guadagno, Fortuna, Materialismo, Possesso, Inizio.* Guadagno e prosperità sono tutto ciò che si prospetta all'orizzonte. Fortuna e pace benediranno il tuo tragitto.

2 DI DENARI — *Parole chiave: Dualità, Allegria, Flessibilità, Goliardia, Incostanza.* La fretta è cattiva consigliera. Se non riesci a gestire più cose contemporaneamente, abbandonane qualcuna prima di farti del male.

3 DI DENARI — *Parole chiave: Artigianato, Arte, Progetto, Talento, Ispirazione.* Porta avanti i tuoi progetti con passione, ma pianificali con cura, se non vuoi rischiare di restare ferito nel processo.

4 DI DENARI — *Parole chiave: Avidità, Parsimonia, Controllo, Eredità, Investimento.* Proteggere i propri spazi è legittimo, ma il controllo possessivo e l'avarizia sono atteggiamenti da cui devi assolutamente tenerti alla larga.

5 DI DENARI — *Parole chiave: Bisogno, Povertà, Lotta, Ostacolo, Freddo.* In momenti di magra, virtù come la generosità e il rispetto possono rimetterti in piedi e renderti ancora più forte di prima.

6 DI DENARI — *Parole chiave: Generosità, Carità, Distribuzione, Empatia, Offerta.* L'altruismo richiede sacrifici, ma le ricompense sono sempre più grandi di qualsiasi cosa si sia dovuto abbandonare.

7 DI DENARI — *Parole chiave: Valutazione, Espansione, Dovere, Sviluppo, Controllo.* Potrà sembrare controintuitivo, ma l'attesa può essere l'atto più produttivo che esista. Non ti affannare e lascia che le situazioni diano i loro frutti.

8 DI DENARI — *Parole chiave: Lavoro, Abitudine, Impegno, Autonomia, Finezza.* La dedizione a un obiettivo è una qualità ammirevole: applicati nel tuo mestiere o nella tua passione per ottenere il massimo ed evitare futuri rimpianti.

9 DI DENARI — *Parole chiave: Prudenza, Indipendenza, Educazione, Sicurezza, Ricchezza.* Emancipazione e indipendenza

sono le linee guida. Le situazioni problematiche si risolveranno man mano che svilupperai abilità secondarie per poterle gestire.

10 DI DENARI — *Parole chiave: Ricchezza, Eredità, Legame, Culmine, Casa.* Sii resiliente. Eredità, tradizioni e tutte le trasmissioni di ricchezze fisiche o immateriali sono sintomo di una sana continuità.

FANTE DI DENARI — *Parole chiave: Sforzo, Studio, Praticità, Curiosità, Esame.* La curiosità è positiva, ma bisogna assicurarsi di non lasciarsi trasportare troppo e non sforzarsi eccessivamente nello studio o nel lavoro.

CAVALIERE DI DENARI — *Parole chiave: Adattabilità, Pragmatismo, Persistenza, Professionalità, Affidabilità.* Concentrati e porta avanti il tuo compito con diligenza per non veder sparire in un batter d'occhio tutto ciò che hai conquistato finora.

RE DI DENARI — *Parole chiave: Affari, Impresa, Denaro, Amministrazione, Maturazione.* Assumi più autorità e responsabilità nel portare avanti i tuoi progetti, e presto potrai accedere ai frutti succulenti del successo.

REGINA DI DENARI — *Parole chiave: Conservazione, Coscienza, Nutrimento, Cuore, Discrezione.* A volte sono necessarie misure severe per preservare ciò che è importante. Abbi particolare cura delle cose e delle persone a te care.

BASTONI

ASSO DI BASTONI — *Parole chiave: Creatività, Originalità, Avventura, Forza, Scintilla.* Che sia positiva o negativa, questa è la scintilla che dà inizio a una nuova avventura, alla fiamma sacra alimentata dal potere della creazione.

2 DI BASTONI — *Parole chiave: Piano, Aspirazione, Slancio, Irrequietezza, Arroganza.* I tuoi progetti traggono beneficio da un'accurata preparazione, ma bada a non alimentare troppo l'aspettativa: l'arroganza si ritorce sempre contro.

3 DI BASTONI — *Parole chiave: Anticipazione, Osservazione, Attenzione, Ritardo, Previsione.* La foga nel perseguire un obiettivo può provocare grossi danni. Le cose sono già in movimento: aspetta il momento migliore per agire.

4 DI BASTONI — *Parole chiave: Celebrazione, Preparazione, Tranquillità, Perfezionismo, Solidità.* Si preannuncia l'arrivo di un'occasione gioiosa, un momento per festeggiare con amici e familiari, o semplicemente un incontro per riportare stabilità.

5 DI BASTONI — *Parole chiave: Competizione, Rivalità, Conflitto, Allenamento, Imitazione.* Una sana competitività è certamente una caratteristica positiva, ma assicurati di sapere per cosa vale la pena combattere.

6 DI BASTONI — *Parole chiave: Vittoria, Fama, Vanità, Diplomazia, Novità.* Celebra il tuo trionfo e non permettere a nessuno di rovinare i festeggiamenti, ma evita di essere eccessivamente zelante.

7 DI BASTONI — *Parole chiave: Difesa, Opposizione, Opinione, Battaglia, Anticon-*

formismo. La battaglia è alle porte. Sentiti libero di far sentire la tua voce, ma preparati a sostenere coi fatti le tue affermazioni.

8 DI BASTONI — *Parole chiave: Velocità, Movimento, Rapidità, Reazione, Spedizione.* Indugiare crea dolore; la stagnazione genera tristezza. Tieni questo pensiero a mente per perseguire le tue imprese con energia e rapidità.

9 DI BASTONI — *Parole chiave: Guardia, Cautela, Tenacia, Soglia, Esperienza.* Qualcosa minaccia il tuo spazio personale, che devi sorvegliare con prudenza. Attenzione, perché spesso i pericoli si presentano in forme ingannevolmente innocue.

10 DI BASTONI — *Parole chiave: Stanchezza, Fatica, Oppressione, Esaurimento, Completamento.* C'è un "peso morto" che dovresti toglierti dalle spalle. Smettila di correre: è arrivato il momento di riposare.

FANTE DI BASTONI — *Parole chiave: Iniziativa, Vitalità, Eccitazione, Giocosità, Rischio.* Non c'è nulla di più sano di un'anima giocosa in cerca di avventure. Attenzione, però: il tuo fuoco è ancora acerbo e rappresenta una sterile difesa dai pericoli del cammino.

CAVALIERE DI BASTONI — *Parole chiave: Coraggio, Slancio, Distanza, Idealismo, Incoscienza.* Avanza con slancio; passa attraverso il fuoco per raggiungere i tuoi obiettivi. Se l'oggetto desiderato è fuori portata, non aver paura di chiedere aiuto per accelerare il processo.

RE DI BASTONI — *Parole chiave: Leadership, Motivazione, Persuasione, Arguzia, Presunzione.* Presunzione e superbia possono sottoporti a grossi rischi. Accetta le tue responsabilità: dopotutto, è proprio questo che fa un vero leader.

REGINA DI BASTONI — *Parole chiave: Carisma, Magnetismo, Sensualità, Ottimismo, Vivacità.* Adotta una combinazione di delicatezza e aggressività: i pilastri della personalità carismatica e sfaccettata che devi incarnare.

SPADE

ASSO DI SPADE — *Parole chiave: Pensiero, Idea, Obiettività, Responsabilità, Convinzione.* Sorvola i problemi con la forza delle nuove idee. Attenzione, però, perché il pensiero cervellotico può portare a una disciplina troppo rigida e a responsabilità eccessive.

2 DI SPADE — *Parole chiave: Duello, Discussione, Dualità, Stallo, Cecità.* Scegli con saggezza il percorso e i tuoi nemici, e fai attenzione alle opzioni troppo allettanti, perché il loro aspetto potrebbe nascondere pericoli inaspettati.

3 DI SPADE — *Parole chiave: Dispiacere, Dolore, Disperazione, Colpa, Rimpianto.* Un evento doloroso o un vecchio rancore bussa ora alla tua porta. Non abbandonarti alla disperazione e affronta il problema stringendo i denti.

4 DI SPADE — *Parole chiave: Recupero, Sonno, Tregua, Ritiro, Pausa.* Non ossessionarti con obiettivi e ambizioni, perché la stabilità della mente è la cosa più importante. Prenditi del tempo per riposare, riflettere e recuperare.

5 DI SPADE — *Parole chiave: Egoismo, Compiacimento, Dominazione, Vendetta, Dramma.* Abbandona l'egoismo, l'orgoglio e il potere. Sii umile e accetta l'aiuto esterno, se necessario, e il tuo regno vedrà finalmente la luce.

6 DI SPADE — *Parole chiave: Viaggio, Fuga, Rinuncia, Espediente, Trasferimento.* Sei da qualche parte tra la partenza e la destinazione. Sentirsi alla deriva è normale quando si è nel bel mezzo di una ricerca, ma presto vedrai la terra all'orizzonte.

7 DI SPADE — *Parole chiave: Furtività, Sotterfugio, Scorciatoia, Spionaggio, Raccolta.* Una minaccia silenziosa si avvicina; qualcuno mente o trama alle tue spalle. In alternativa, potresti essere tu a dover tramare per superare il problema.

8 DI SPADE — *Parole chiave: Limite, Letargo, Paralisi, Trappola, Impedimento.* C'è una situazione di stasi, forse causata da un trauma passato. Condividere il carico potrebbe essere il modo giusto per superare il blocco.

9 DI SPADE — *Parole chiave: Angoscia, Disperazione, Incertezza, Oscurità, Dubbio.* Stai sperimentando dubbi improvvisi, sensi di colpa, ansie o comportamenti ossessivi. Discuti apertamente il problema per spogliarlo della sua carica negativa.

10 DI SPADE — *Parole chiave: Afflizione, Blocco, Desolazione, Paura, Fine.* Non aggrapparti alle memorie di un passato che non tornerà. Non disperare: la perdita non è che il preludio della trascendenza.

FANTE DI SPADE — *Parole chiave: Impazienza, Intelligenza, Genio, Calcolo, Aiuto.* Sii vigile e proteggi ciò che ami con arguzia, ma ricorda di guardare oltre il tuo perimetro per imparare ancora e migliorare te stesso.

CAVALIERE DI SPADE — *Parole chiave: Destrezza, Impazienza, Valore, Fretta, Franchezza.* Rifletti prima di agire e prendi decisioni onorevoli. Essere scaltro e impaziente ti fa saltare alle conclusioni, a volte.

RE DI SPADE — *Parole chiave: Razionalità, Analisi, Precisione, Tattica, Concentrazione.* Afferma te stesso ed escogita una maniera per assumere il controllo della situazione attuale. Se combattere contro qualcuno che ti è vicino è l'unica soluzione logica, non esitare.

REGINA DI SPADE — *Parole chiave: Schiettezza, Strategia, Rigore, Concisione, Disciplina.* Le tue azioni devono essere rapide e dirette. Apri la bocca solo per favorire i meritevoli o punire gli indegni, senza vie di mezzo.

YŌKAI TAROT

INTRODUCCIÓN

Quien no esté familiarizado con los *yōkai* tenderá a identificarlos como una colección banal de monstruos y fantasmas exóticos, pero nada podría estar más lejos de la verdad. De hecho, estas criaturas representan una parte integral del patrimonio cultural japonés y derivan directamente de su religión indígena, el sintoísmo, que apoya la tesis animista según la cual las entidades naturales -e incluso algunos objetos- están dotados de alma e intelecto. Esta creencia da vida a un mundo mágico impregnado de sensibilidad y significado, donde cada cosa posee una voluntad propia con la que es posible interactuar.

En pocas palabras, los *yōkai* representan la personificación de todos los fenómenos de la realidad y, por lo tanto, relacionarse con ellos significa tratar con la realidad misma.

Visto desde esta perspectiva, la combinación con un instrumento de exploración como el del Tarot puede resultar obvia y natural, ya que define el punto de encuentro entre dos mecanismos perfectamente complementarios: la manifestación del mundo como interlocutor inmanente y el poder comunicativo de los 78 Arcanos que abren un diálogo que puede ayudarte a comprender y afrontar mejor este mundo.

Aquí, el Yōkai Tarot es precisamente el fruto de esta combinación tan especial.

LECTURA DEL TORII

Este esquema, diseñado específicamente para el Yōkai Tarot, tiene la forma de un *torii*, los famosos portales ubicados en los ingresos de los santuarios sintoístas. El *torii* representa un umbral entre los reinos terrenal y espiritual y, como tal, introduce al lector a niveles superiores de conciencia. Esta lectura debe usarse específicamente como guía a la meditación: construye tu *torii* pieza por pieza, reflexionando sobre los distintos niveles, para luego atravesarlo y alcanzar la iluminación.

1-2: Los principios en la base del viaje; los valores que deben guiar cada uno de tus pasos. Estos cimientos soportarán el peso de la construcción que está por surgir y servirán como pilares conceptuales para la nueva estructura.

3-4: Lo que necesitas dejar ir para continuar; episodios, personas o ideas que ahora podrás "asentar" en la solidez de los pilares recién erigidos. Lo que alguna vez consideraste como una carga debe superarse y transformarse en bloques de experiencia sobre los cuales puedas seguir construyendo. La liberación te vuelve ligero y libre para ascender.

5-6: La epifanía al final del viaje; el punto de inflexión de tu conciencia. Los nuevos valores te han permitido soltar los asuntos terrenales y, al liberarlos, se convirtieron en valiosas lecciones. Ahora tu mente está lista para volar entre las verdades celestiales de modo de poder completar tu evolución.

ARCANOS MAYORES

0 · EL LOCO — *Palabras clave: Libertad, Espontaneidad, Inocencia, Locura, Ingenio.* Caminar con la cabeza en alto te permite tener una buena visión del horizonte, pero te impide notar lo que hay bajo tus pies. La aventura es a la vez liberadora y peligrosa: ¡disfrútala con precaución!

I · EL MAGO — *Palabras clave: Voluntad, Habilidad, Ambición, Engaño, Mentiras.* Dedícate a tus proyectos y perfecciona tus múltiples talentos, pero luego asegúrate de tomar una dirección definitiva y de no dar vueltas en vano.

II · LA PAPISA — *Palabras clave: Sabiduría, Intuición, Secreto, Introspección, Severidad.* Confía en la certeza de que fuerzas superiores a ti están trabajando para dirigir tu camino. Agudiza tu intuición para identificar las señales más crípticas y confusas.

III · LA EMPERATRIZ — *Palabras clave: Abundancia, Fertilidad, Elegancia, Belleza, Protección.* El amor y la pertenencia son las cualidades a encarnar: te conducirán a la riqueza y a la fecundidad, pero también a la nobleza del alma, tan necesaria para poner todo en beneficio de los demás.

IV · EL EMPERADOR — *Palabras clave: Poder, Autoridad, Disciplina, Experiencia, Precisión.* Hazte cargo de la situación y contrólala; establece los límites y defiéndelos. Sin embargo, asegúrate de que te respeten en lugar de que te teman: la severidad y la crueldad son dos cosas muy diferentes.

V · EL PAPA — *Palabras clave: Conocimiento, Inspiración, Fe, Conformidad, Jerarquía.* Analiza a fondo la situación, porque podría ser distinta de lo que parece. Sigue las tradiciones e intégrate en la sociedad, pero no te pierdas por completo al hacerlo.

VI · LOS AMANTES — *Palabras clave: Alegría, Pasión, Unión, Deseo, Elección.* A veces son necesarios algunos sacrificios para establecer un vínculo significativo. Si se hace una elección desde el corazón, incluso la carga más pesada valdrá la pena.

VII · EL CARRO — *Palabras clave: Acción, Progreso, Energía, Viaje, Confianza.* Afronta las cosas directamente. Aborda tus proyectos, tus problemas y tus miedos con determinación y acepta tus responsabilidades: seguramente serás recompensado.

VIII · LA FUERZA — *Palabras clave: Coraje, Resistencia, Compostura, Paciencia, Serenidad.* La verdadera fuerza reside en un espíritu indomable; una buena postura siempre le gana a una apariencia desgarbada. El carácter es lo que realmente necesitas para manejar las situaciones "resbaladizas".

IX · EL ERMITAÑO — *Palabras clave: Orientación, Meditación, Prudencia, Humildad, Retiro.* Reclúyete en tu intimidad para meditar y alcanzar la iluminación; busca dentro de ti la orientación que necesitas y avanza con prudencia para encontrar un paso entre las montañas.

X · LA RUEDA — *Palabras clave: Destino, Revolución, Repetición, Alternancia, Suerte.* No interfieras con los ciclos naturales: las cosas cambian a su propio ritmo, aceptarlo y seguir el flujo es la mejor manera de evitar ser aplastado por el infinito giro de la Rueda.

XI · LA JUSTICIA — *Palabras clave: Equidad, Equilibrio, Valor, Lógica, Insensibilidad.* Actúa siempre como si un observador imparcial te estuviera vigilando, examinando tus acciones. Lo justo es siempre una prioridad, independientemente de los resultados.

XII · EL COLGADO — *Palabras clave: Trascendencia, Inversión, Perspectiva, Aceptación, Epifanía.* Ten cuidado con las trampas en el camino y no te lances de cabeza a las situaciones. Es posible que necesites revertir tu perspectiva actual para llegar a la solución.

XIII · LA MUERTE — *Palabras clave: Fin, Paso, Transformación, Limpieza, Irreversibilidad.* Enfrentar y procesar lo irreversible es la única manera de superar algunas cosas. No dejes que el pasado te atormente: el final es sólo la transición hacia un nuevo comienzo.

XIV · LA TEMPLANZA — *Palabras clave: Mediación, Adaptación, Compromiso, Armonía, Regeneración.* Practica el equilibrio interior mediando los impulsos y combinando cuidadosamente las fuerzas opuestas dentro de ti. La mezcla iniciará el proceso de curación que necesitas ahora.

XV · EL DIABLO — *Palabras clave: Tentación, Obsesión, Egoísmo, Indulgencia, Tabú.* No tengas miedo de satisfacer tus pasiones y nunca te abstengas de los placeres de la vida. En cambio, ten cuidado con los excesos, ya que corren el riesgo de arruinar el disfrute en sí.

XVI · LA TORRE — *Palabras clave: Conmoción, Ruina, Destrucción, Liberación, Caos.* Incluso las mejores estructuras pueden caer debido a acontecimientos inesperados. El colapso es doloroso, pero las lecciones serán fundamentales para reconstruir un sistema más fuerte y eficiente.

XVII · LA ESTRELLA — *Palabras clave: Esperanza, Claridad, Tranquilidad, Pureza, Dirección.* Ten fe: todas las piezas encajarán en el lugar correcto. Mantén este sentimiento cerca de tu corazón como protección mientras persigues el claro sueño que brilla en la oscuridad de la noche.

XVIII · LA LUNA — *Palabras clave: Misterio, Ilusión, Subconsciente, Romanticismo, Ocultismo.* Este es el momento de utilizar la intuición en lugar de la simple racionalidad. El subconsciente a veces puede engañar, pero la razón por sí sola no puede abrir todas las puertas.

XIX · EL SOL — *Palabras clave: Verdad, Gloria, Felicidad, Honestidad, Exuberancia.* Invierte nuevas energías con entusiasmo. Disfruta de la luz del sol, pero nunca te detengas a mirarlo directamente, ya que ciega a quienes lo miran con arrogancia.

XX · EL JUICIO — *Palabras clave: Despertar, Revelación, Redención, Surgimiento, Liberación.* No importa qué tan lejos corras o qué tan bien te puedas esconder, no podrás escapar del juicio. El cambio está en camino; la revelación traerá la revolución.

XXI · EL MUNDO — *Palabras clave: Cumplimiento, Realización, Integración, Recompensa, Satisfacción.* Un poco de movimiento es fundamental para no estancarse en una posición privilegiada, pero mantén a raya la arrogancia y la exuberancia, o el mundo que ahora descansa sobre tus hombros se derrumbará sobre ti.

COPAS

AS DE COPAS — *Palabras clave: Emoción, Memoria, Cuidado, Apertura, Paz.* Un augurio positivo aleja las enfermedades y la mala suerte. Hay una explosión de serenidad, alegría, nutrición y abundancia en tu vida.

2 DE COPAS — *Palabras clave: Atracción, Afinidad, Reciprocidad, Acuerdo, Pacto.* Reencuéntrate con tu pareja o supera por fin la timidez para poder expresarle tus sentimientos a la persona que amas. Si hay una disputa, puede que sea el momento de resolverla.

3 DE COPAS — *Palabras clave: Comunión, Frivolidad, Danza, Entusiasmo, Embriaguez.* Los resultados positivos están a la vuelta de la esquina: es hora de poner fin a los conflictos y de entablar nuevas amistades. ¡Disfruta de estos días felices, pero no te excedas con las celebraciones!

4 DE COPAS — *Palabras clave: Aburrimiento, Apatía, Desencanto, Distracción, Expectativa.* Algo no funciona. Es posible

que estés demasiado distraído para darte cuenta de una oportunidad, o tal vez simplemente estés aburrido. Es necesario tomar medidas para restablecer una sed saludable de vida.

5 DE COPAS — *Palabras clave: Lamento, Pérdida, Rechazo, Desesperación, Arrepentimiento.* No todas las esperanzas están perdidas, pero es difícil poder ver la luz al final del túnel si le das la espalda a las nuevas oportunidades. Lo que falta no debería arruinar lo que todavía está allí.

6 DE COPAS — *Palabras clave: Nostalgia, Ausencia, Amistad, Altruismo, Seguridad.* Encuentra un refugio, un espacio seguro e íntimo donde puedas resguardarte cuando llegue el mal tiempo. Utiliza esta protección y extiéndela a otros mientras esperas un nuevo día soleado.

7 DE COPAS — *Palabras clave: Fantasía, Visión, Variedad, Selección, Envidia.* La selección es un aspecto fundamental, así que considera todas las opciones cuidadosamente. Sueña, pero con humildad: un apetito sin fondo te puede empantanar.

8 DE COPAS — *Palabras clave: Liberación, Renuncia, Timidez, Previsión, Aventura.* Sal de tu zona de confort. El viaje puede ser largo, difícil o solitario, pero superar los miedos y la timidez es la única manera de descubrir novedades maravillosas.

9 DE COPAS — *Palabras clave: Satisfacción, Placer, Virtud, Sensualidad, Saturación.* La satisfacción es grande, pero a la larga la riqueza acumulada puede resultar perjudicial. Es posible que necesites soltar algunas trabas para resurgir y respirar.

10 DE COPAS — *Palabras clave: Éxito, Conclusión, Reconocimiento, Familia, Descanso.* Una situación problemática está a punto de resolverse y el resultado positivo llega con regalos para ti y para las personas que más amas. Disfruta estos momentos.

SOTA DE COPAS — *Palabras clave: Receptividad, Dulzura, Bondad, Percepción, Gracia.* Cualidades como la bondad y la gracia siempre pueden resultar útiles, independientemente de los méritos de la persona a quien van dirigidas.

CABALLERO DE COPAS — *Palabras clave: Seducción, Adulación, Coraje, Temperamento, Calidez.* Avanza sin miedo hacia lugares fascinantes, misteriosos y prohibidos. Sigue con valentía el camino trazado por tu corazón.

REY DE COPAS — *Palabras clave: Lealtad, Compostura, Calma, Cariño, Simpatía.* Es importante acercarse a los demás con una actitud amistosa, pero es igualmente esencial responder adecuadamente a los atropellos.

REINA DE COPAS — *Palabras clave: Sensibilidad, Tolerancia, Perdón, Ternura, Apoyo.* Baja la cabeza, evita el contacto visual y sigue adelante. A veces es necesario tolerar, perdonar e incluso olvidar a una persona o una situación para evitar ser herido.

OROS

AS DE OROS — *Palabras clave: Ganancias, Suerte, Materialismo, Posesión, Comienzo.* Ganancias y prosperidad es todo lo que se vislumbra en el horizonte. La suerte y la paz bendecirán tu camino.

2 DE OROS — *Palabras clave: Dualidad, Alegría, Flexibilidad, Bohemia, Inconstancia.* La prisa es mala consejera. Si no puedes manejar varias cosas a la vez, abandona alguna de ellas antes de lastimarte.

3 DE OROS — *Palabras clave: Artesanía, Arte, Proyecto, Talento, Inspiración.* Lleva adelante tus proyectos con pasión, pero planifícalos con cuidado si no quieres correr el riesgo de salir lastimado en el proceso.

4 DE OROS — *Palabras clave: Avaricia, Ahorro, Control, Herencia, Inversión.* Proteger los propios espacios es legítimo, pero el control posesivo y la codicia son actitudes de las que debes mantenerte alejado.

5 DE OROS — *Palabras clave: Necesidad, Pobreza, Lucha, Obstáculo, Frío.* En tiempos difíciles, virtudes como la generosidad y el respeto pueden ayudarte a recuperarte y hacerte aún más fuerte que antes.

6 DE OROS — *Palabras clave: Generosidad, Caridad, Distribución, Empatía, Ofrecimiento.* El altruismo requiere sacrificio, pero las recompensas son siempre mayores que cualquier cosa a la que hayas tenido que renunciar.

7 DE OROS — *Palabras clave: Evaluación, Expansión, Deber, Desarrollo, Control.* Puede parecer contradictorio, pero la espera puede ser el acto más productivo que exista. No te preocupes y deja que las situaciones den sus frutos.

8 DE OROS — *Palabras clave: Trabajo, Hábito, Compromiso, Autonomía, Delicadeza.* La dedicación a una meta es una cualidad admirable: aplícate a tu profesión o a tu pasión para sacar el máximo provecho y así evitar arrepentimientos futuros.

9 DE OROS — *Palabras clave: Prudencia, Independencia, Educación, Seguridad,*

Riqueza. La emancipación y la independencia son los lineamentos guías. Las situaciones problemáticas se resolverán solas a medida que desarrolles habilidades secundarias para poder manejarlas.

10 DE OROS — *Palabras clave: Riqueza, Herencia, Vínculo, Culminación, Hogar.* Sé resiliente. La herencia, las tradiciones y todas las transmisiones de riquezas físicas o inmateriales son síntoma de una sana continuidad.

SOTA DE OROS — *Palabras clave: Esfuerzo, Estudio, Practicidad, Curiosidad, Examen.* La curiosidad es positiva, pero debes asegurarte de no dejarte llevar demasiado y de no esforzarte excesivamente en tus estudios o trabajo.

CABALLERO DE OROS — *Palabras clave: Adaptabilidad, Pragmatismo, Persistencia, Profesionalismo, Fiabilidad.* Concéntrate y realiza tu tarea con diligencia para no ver desaparecer en un abrir y cerrar de ojos todo lo que has conseguido hasta ahora.

REY DE OROS — *Palabras clave: Negocios, Empresa, Dinero, Administración,*

Maduración. Asume una mayor autoridad y responsabilidad en la realización de tus proyectos y pronto podrás acceder a los suculentos frutos del éxito.

REINA DE OROS — *Palabras clave: Conservación, Conciencia, Nutrición, Corazón, Discreción.* A veces son necesarias medidas severas para preservar lo que es importante. Cuida especialmente las cosas y a las personas que amas.

BASTOS

AS DE BASTOS — *Palabras clave: Creatividad, Originalidad, Aventura, Fuerza, Chispa.* Ya sea positiva o negativa, esta es la chispa que inicia una nueva aventura, la llama sagrada alimentada por el poder de la creación.

2 DE BASTOS — *Palabras clave: Plan, Aspiración, Impulso, Inquietud, Arrogancia.* Tus proyectos se benefician de una preparación cuidadosa, pero ten cuidado de no generar demasiadas expectativas: la arrogancia siempre resulta contraproducente.

3 DE BASTOS — *Palabras clave: Anticipación, Observación, Atención, Retraso, Previsión.* La prisa por perseguir un objetivo puede causar grandes daños. Las cosas ya están en marcha: espera el mejor momento para actuar.

4 DE BASTOS — *Palabras clave: Celebración, Preparación, Tranquilidad, Perfeccionismo, Solidez.* Se preanuncia la llegada de una ocasión alegre, un momento para regocijarse con amigos y familiares o simplemente una reunión para restablecer la estabilidad.

5 DE BASTOS — *Palabras clave: Competencia, Rivalidad, Conflicto, Entrenamiento, Imitación.* Una sana competitividad es ciertamente un rasgo positivo, pero asegúrate de saber bien por cuáles cosas vale la pena luchar.

6 DE BASTOS — *Palabras clave: Victoria, Fama, Vanidad, Diplomacia, Novedades.* Celebra tu triunfo y no dejes que nadie arruine la celebración, pero evita ser demasiado celoso.

7 DE BASTOS — *Palabras clave: Defensa, Oposición, Opinión, Batalla, Incon-*

formismo. La batalla está sobre nosotros. Siéntete libre de hacer oír tu voz, pero prepárate para respaldar tus afirmaciones con hechos.

8 DE BASTOS — *Palabras clave: Velocidad, Movimiento, Rapidez, Reacción, Expedición*. Persistir crea dolor; el estancamiento genera tristeza. Ten este pensamiento en mente para continuar persiguiendo tus proyectos con energía y velocidad.

9 DE BASTOS — *Palabras clave: Guardia, Precaución, Tenacidad, Umbral, Experiencia*. Algo amenaza tu espacio personal, que debes proteger con precaución. Ten cuidado, porque los peligros a menudo se presentan en formas engañosamente inofensivas.

10 DE BASTOS — *Palabras clave: Cansancio, Fatiga, Opresión, Agotamiento, Desenlace*. Hay un "peso muerto" que debes quitarte de tus espaldas. Deja de correr: es hora de descansar.

SOTA DE BASTOS — *Palabras clave: Iniciativa, Vitalidad, Entusiasmo, Alegría, Riesgo*. No hay nada más saludable que un alma juguetona en busca de aventuras. Pero ten cuidado: tu fuego aún es inmaduro y representa una defensa estéril contra los peligros del viaje.

CABALLERO DE BASTOS — *Palabras clave: Coraje, Impulso, Distancia, Idealismo, Inconsciencia.* Avanza con impulso; llénate de entusiasmo y pasión para lograr tus objetivos. Si aquello que deseas está fuera de tu alcance, no temas pedir ayuda para acelerar el proceso.

REY DE BASTOS — *Palabras clave: Liderazgo, Motivación, Persuasión, Ingenio, Vanidad.* La presunción y el orgullo pueden someterte a grandes riesgos. Acepta tus responsabilidades; después de todo, esto es lo que hace un verdadero líder.

REINA DE BASTOS — *Palabras clave: Carisma, Magnetismo, Sensualidad, Optimismo, Vivacidad.* Adopta una combinación de delicadeza y espíritu combativo: los pilares de la personalidad carismática y multifacética que debes encarnar.

AS DE ESPADAS — *Palabras clave: Pensamiento, Idea, Objetividad, Responsabilidad, Convicción.* Supera los problemas con la fuerza de las nuevas ideas. Sin embargo, ten cuidado, porque los pensamientos extremadamente racionales pueden conducirte a una disciplina demasiado rígida y a responsabilidades excesivas.

2 DE ESPADAS — *Palabras clave: Duelo, Discusión, Dualidad, Estancamiento, Ceguera.* Elige sabiamente tu camino y tus enemigos, y ten cuidado con las opciones que sean demasiado tentadoras, ya que su apariencia puede ocultar peligros inesperados.

3 DE ESPADAS — *Palabras clave: Disgusto, Dolor, Desesperación, Culpa, Arrepentimiento..* Un acontecimiento doloroso o un viejo rencor ahora llama a tu puerta. No te desesperes y afronta el problema con todas tus fuerzas.

4 DE ESPADAS — *Palabras clave: Recuperación, Sueño, Tregua, Retiro, Pausa.* No te obsesiones con metas y ambiciones, porque la estabilidad mental es lo más importante. Tómate el tiempo para descansar, reflexionar y recuperarte.

5 DE ESPADAS — *Palabras clave: Egoísmo, Complacencia, Dominación, Venganza, Drama.* Abandona el egoísmo, el orgullo y el poder. Sé humilde y si es necesario, acepta la ayuda externa y tu reino finalmente verá la luz.

6 DE ESPADAS — *Palabras clave: Viaje, Escape, Renuncia, Conveniente, Traslado.* Ahora estás en algún sitio entre el lugar del que partiste y el destino al que te gustaría llegar. Sentirse a la deriva es normal cuando estás en medio de una búsqueda, pero pronto verás tierra en el horizonte.

7 DE ESPADAS — *Palabras clave: Furtivo, Subterfugio, Atajo, Espionaje, Recopilación.* Se acerca una amenaza silenciosa; alguien miente o conspira a tus espaldas. Alternativamente, puedes ser tú quien tenga que tramar una solución al problema.

8 DE ESPADAS — *Palabras clave: Límite, Letargo, Parálisis, Trampa, Impedimen-*

to. Hay una situación de estancamiento, quizas provocada por un trauma del pasado. Compartir la carga podría ser la forma correcta de superar el bloqueo.

9 DE ESPADAS — *Palabras clave: Angustia, Desesperación, Incertidumbre, Oscuridad, Duda.* Estás experimentando dudas repentinas, culpa, ansiedad o comportamientos obsesivos. Discute el problema abiertamente para despojarlo de su carga negativa.

10 DE ESPADAS — *Palabras clave: Aflicción, Bloqueo, Desolación, Miedo, Fin.* No te aferres a los recuerdos de un pasado que no volverá. No te desesperes: la pérdida no es más que el preludio de la trascendencia.

SOTA DE ESPADAS — *Palabras clave: Impaciencia, Inteligencia, Genio, Cálculo, Ayuda.* Estate atento y protege lo que amas con ingenio, pero recuerda mirar más allá de tus narices para aprender más y mejorarte a ti mismo.

CABALLERO DE ESPADAS — *Palabras clave: Destreza, Impaciencia, Valor,*

Prisa, Franqueza. Piensa siempre antes de actuar y toma decisiones honorables. Ser astuto e impaciente a veces te hace sacar conclusiones precipitadas.

REY DE ESPADAS — *Palabras clave: Racionalidad, Análisis, Precisión, Táctica, Concentración.* Afírmate y encuentra una manera de tomar el control de la situación actual. Si enfrentarte con alguien cercano a ti es la única solución lógica, no lo dudes.

REINA DE ESPADAS — *Palabras clave: Sinceridad, Estrategia, Rigor, Concisión, Disciplina.* Tus acciones deben ser rápidas y directas. Abre la boca sólo para favorecer a quien lo merece o para castigar al injusto, sin vías intermedias.

YŌKAI TAROT

INTRODUÇÃO

Quem não está familiarizado com os *yōkai* tende a os identificar como uma mera coleção de monstros exóticos e fantasmas, mas nada poderia estar mais longe da verdade. Na realidade, estos seres representam uma parte essencial da herança cultural japonesa, e derivam diretamente da sua religião indígena, o xintoísmo, que defende a tese animista de que entidades naturais – e até mesmo alguns objetos – possuem alma e inteligência. Esta crença dá origem a um mundo mágico permeado de consciência e significado, onde tudo tem a sua própria vontade e é possível interagir com ela.

Em suma, os *yōkai* representam a personificação de todos os fenómenos da realidade e, portanto, lidar com eles significa lidar com a própria realidade.

Nesta perspetiva, a combinação com uma ferramenta de investigação como os Tarots parece bastante evidente e natural, pois define o ponto de encontro entre dois mecanismos perfeitamente complementares: a manifestação do mundo como interlocutor imanente e o poder comunicativo do 78 Arcanos, para iniciar um diálogo que lhe dê a possibilidade de compreendê-lo e enfrentá-lo. O Yōkai Tarot é precisamente o resultado desta combinação especial.

LANÇAMENTO DO TORII

Este Lançamento, pensado especificamente para o Yōkai Tarot, tem a forma de um *torii*, os famosos portais localizados na entrada dos santuários xintoístas. O *torii* representa um limiar entre os reinos terreno e espiritual e, como tal, introduz o leitor a níveis mais elevados de consciência. Este Lançamento deve ser usado especificamente como guia para a meditação: construa o seu *torii* pedaço por pedaço, refletindo sobre os vários níveis, para depois atravessá-lo e alcançar a iluminação.

1-2: Os princípios fundamentais da jornada; os valores que devem guiar cada um dos seus passos. Estas bases irão sustentar o peso da construção que está prestes a erguer-se, e serão os pilares conceptuais da nova estrutura.

3-4: O que precisa deixar para trás para progredir; episódios, pessoas ou ideias que agora pode "consolidar" sobre a solidez dos pilares recém-erigidos. O que uma vez foi considerado um fardo deve ser superado e transformado em blocos de experiência sobre os quais continuar a construir. O ato de soltar torna-o leve e livre para ascender.

5-6: A epifania no final da jornada; o ponto de viragem da sua consciência. Os novos valores permitiram-lhe deixar para trás as preocupações mundanas e, ao soltá-las, estas transformaram-se em preciosas lições. Agora a sua mente está pronta para elevar-se entre as verdades celestiais, para completar a sua evolução.

ARCANOS MAIORES

0 · O LOUCO — *Palavras-chave: Liberdade, Espontaneidade, Inocência, Loucura, Ingenuidade.* Caminhar de cabeça erguida permite-lhe ter uma boa visão do horizonte, mas impede-lhe de notar o que está abaixo dos seus pés. A aventura é tanto libertadora como perigosa: aproveita-a com cuidado!

I · O MAGO — *Palavras-chave: Vontade, Habilidade, Ambição, Engano, Mentira.* Dedique-se aos seus projetos e aperfeiçoe os seus numerosos talentos, mas depois assegure-se de tomar uma direção clara e não se perder em indecisões.

II · A SACERDOTISA — *Palavras-chave: Sabedoria, Intuição, Confidencialidade, Introspeção, Severidade.* Confie na certeza de que existem forças superiores que estão em ação para orientar o seu caminho. Aguce o instinto para identificar os sinais mais enigmáticos e confusos.

III · A IMPERATRIZ — *Palavras-chave: Abundância, Fertilidade, Elegância, Be-*

leza, Proteção. Amor e sentimento de pertença são as qualidades a manifestar: estas conduzir-lhe-ão à riqueza e à fertilidade, mas também à nobreza de caráter necessária para se colocar completamente ao serviço dos outros.

IV · O IMPERADOR — *Palavras-chave: Poder, Autoridade, Disciplina, Experiência, Precisão.* Assuma o controle da situação; estabeleça os limites e defenda-os. Contudo, certifique-se de ser respeitado em vez de temido – severidade e crueldade são dois coisas muito diferentes.

V · O HIEROFANTE — *Palavras-chave: Conhecimento, Inspiração, Fé, Conformidade, Hierarquia.* Analise cuidadosamente a situação, pois pode haver mais do que aparenta. Siga as tradições e integre-se na sociedade, mas não perca completamente a sua própria natureza ao fazê-lo.

VI · OS ENAMORADOS — *Palavras-chave: Alegria, Paixão, União, Desejo, Escolha.* Por vezes os sacrifícios são necessários para estabelecer um vínculo significativo. Se uma escolha for feita com o coração, até mesmo o fardo mais pesado valerá a pena carregar.

VII · O CARRO — *Palavras-chave: Ação, Progresso, Energia, Viagem, Confiança.* Enfrente diretamente as coisas. Aborde os projetos, os problemas e os medos com determinação e assuma as suas responsabilidades – certamente será recompensado.

VIII · A FORÇA — *Palavras-chave: Coragem, Resistência, Autocontrolo, Paciência, Serenidade.* A verdadeira força reside num espírito indomável; uma boa atitude sempre vence a mera agitação. O carácter é o segredo para superar situações desafiantes.

IX · O EREMITA — *Palavras-chave: Guia, Meditação, Cautela, Humildade, Retiro.* Retire-se para a sua intimidade para meditar e alcançar a iluminação; busque dentro de si a orientação que precisa e siga em frente com cautela para encontrar um caminho entre as montanhas.

X · A RODA — *Palavras-chave: Destino, Revolução, Repetição, Alternância, Sorte.* Não interfira com os ciclos naturais: as coisas mudam no seu próprio ritmo, e aceitar e seguir o fluxo é a melhor maneira de evitar de ser esmagado pelo interminável girar da Roda.

XI · A JUSTIÇA — *Palavras-chave: Equidade, Equilíbrio, Valor, Lógica, Insensibilidade.* Comporte-se sempre como se um observador imparcial o vigiasse, avaliando as suas ações. A honestidade é sempre uma prioridade, independentemente dos resultados.

XII · O ENFORCADO — *Palavras-chave: Transcendência, Inversão, Perspetiva, Aceitação, Epifania.* Esteja atento às armadilhas ao longo do caminho e não mergulhar de cabeça nas situações. Talvez seja necessário inverter a perspetiva atual para chegar à solução.

XIII · A MORTE — *Palavras-chave: Fim, Passagem, Transformação, Limpeza, Irreversibilidade.* Lidar com o que é irreversível e elaborá-lo é a única maneira de superá-lo. Não deixe que o passado o atormente: o fim é apenas a transição para um novo começo.

XIV · A TEMPERANÇA — *Palavras-chave: Mediação, Adaptação, Equilíbrio, Harmonia, Regeneração.* Pratique o equilíbrio interior, medeie os impulsos e misture com cuidado as forças opostas dentro de si. Esta mistura ativará o processo de cura do qual precisa agora.

XV · O DIABO — *Palavras-chave: Tentação, Obsessão, Egoísmo, Prazer, Tabu.* Não tenha medo de desfrutar das suas paixões e nunca se prive dos prazeres da vida. Cuidado com os excessos, pois podem arruinar o próprio prazer.

XVI · A TORRE — *Palavras-chave: Choque, Ruína, Destruição, Libertação, Caos.* Mesmo as melhores estruturas podem desmoronar, devido a eventos imprevistos. A queda é dolorosa, mas a lição será fundamental para reconstruir um sistema mais forte e eficiente.

XVII · A ESTRELA — *Palavras-chave: Esperança, Claridade, Tranquilidade, Pureza, Direção.* Tem confiança: todas as peças voltarão ao lugar certo. Guarde este sentimento próximo ao coração, como proteção, enquanto persegue o sonho luminoso que brilha na escuridão do céu noturno.

XVIII · A LUA — *Palavras-chave: Mistério, Ilusão, Subconsciente, Romantismo, Ocultismo.* Chegou o momento de usar a intuição em vez de apenas a racionalidade. O subconsciente às vezes pode enganar, mas a razão não consegue abrir todas as portas sozinha.

XIX · O SOL — *Palavras-chave: Verdade, Glória, Felicidade, Honestidade, Exuberância.* Invista novas energias com entusiasmo. Desfrute à luz do sol, mas nunca olhe diretamente para ele, pois ele cega aqueles que o enfrentam com arrogância.

XX · O JULGAMENTO — *Palavras-chave: Despertar, Revelação, Redenção, Renascimento, Libertação.* Não importa quão longe corra ou quão bem se esconda: ninguém pode escapar ao julgamento. A mudança está a chegar; a revelação trará a revolução.

XXI · O MUNDO — *Palavras-chave: Prazer, Realização, Integração, Recompensa, Satisfação.* Um pouco de movimento é essencial para não ficar estagnado numa posição privilegiada, mas controle a arrogância e a exuberância, caso contrário o mundo que se apoia nos seus ombros virá abaixo.

COPAS

ÁS DE COPAS — *Palavras-chave: Emoção, Lembrança, Cura, Abertura, Paz.* Um presságio positivo afasta doenças e má sorte. Uma explosão de serenidade, alegria, energia e abundância inunda a sua vida.

2 DE COPAS — *Palavras-chave: Atração, Afinidade, Reciprocidade, Acordo, Pacto.* Reconecte-se com o seu parceiro ou finalmente supere a timidez para expressar os seus sentimentos à pessoa amada. Se houver um conflito em curso, pode ser hora de resolvê-lo.

3 DE COPAS — *Palavras-chave: Comunhão, Frivolidade, Dança, Entusiasmo, Intoxicação.* Os resultados positivos estão ao virar da esquina: é hora de resolver os conflitos e estabelecer novas amizades. Aproveite estes dias felizes, mas não exagere nas celebrações!

4 DE COPAS — *Palavras-chave: Tédio, Apatia, Desencanto, Distração, Expectativa.* Algo está errado. Pode estar demasiado distraído para notar uma oportunidade ou talvez esteja simplesmente cansado. É necessário agir para renovar uma vontade de viver saudável.

5 DE COPAS — *Palavras-chave: Arrependimento, Perda, Rejeição, Desespero, Remorso.* Nem todas as esperanças estão perdidas, mas é difícil ver a luz no final do túnel quando se vira as costas para novas oportunidades. O que está a faltar não deve arruinar o que ainda possui.

6 DE COPAS — *Palavras-chave: Saudade, Falta, Amizade, Altruísmo, Segurança.* Encontre um refúgio, um espaço seguro e íntimo para se abrigar quando a tempestade chegar. Use esta proteção e estenda-a aos outros enquanto aguarda por um novo dia de sol.

7 DE COPAS — *Palavras-chave: Fantasia, Visão, Variedade, Seleção, Inveja.* A seleção é um aspeto fundamental, então avalie atentamente todas as opções. Sonhe, mas com humildade: um apetite insaciável pode-o deixar estagnado.

8 DE COPAS — *Palavras-chave: Libertação, Renúncia, Timidez, Visão do futuro, Aventura.* Abandone a sua zona de conforto. A via-

gem pode ser longa, difícil ou solitária, mas vencer os medos e a timidez é a única maneira de descobrir novidades maravilhosas.

9 DE COPAS — *Palavras-chave: Satisfação, Prazer, Virtude, Sensualidade, Saciedade.* A satisfação é grande, mas a longo prazo a riqueza acumulada pode ser prejudicial. Talvez seja necessário deixar algum peso para emergir e respirar.

10 DE COPAS — *Palavras-chave: Sucesso, Conclusão, Reconhecimento, Família, Descanso.* Uma situação problemática está prestes a ser resolvida, e o resultado positivo traz dádivas para si e para aqueles que lhe são queridos. Desfrute destes momentos.

VALETE DE COPAS — *Palavras-chave: Recetividade, Doçura, Gentileza, Perceção, Graciosidade.* Qualidades como gentileza e elegância podem sempre ser úteis, independentemente dos méritos da pessoa a quem são dirigidas.

CAVALEIRO DE COPAS — *Palavras-chave: Sedução, Adulação, Encorajamento, Temperamento, Calor.* Avance sem medo em direção a lugares fascinantes, misteriosos e proibidos. Siga corajosamente o caminho delineado pelo seu coração.

REI DE COPAS — *Palavras-chave: Lealdade, Autocontrolo, Calma, Afeto, Simpatia.* É importante abordar os outros com uma atitude amigável, mas também é fundamental responder adequadamente aos abusos.

RAINHA DE COPAS — *Palavras-chave: Sensibilidade, Tolerância, Perdão, Ternura, Apoio.* Baixe a cabeça, evite o contato visual e siga em frente. Às vezes é necessário tolerar, perdoar e até mesmo esquecer uma pessoa ou uma situação para evitar ser ferido.

OUROS

ÁS DE OUROS — *Palavras-chave: Ganhos, Sorte, Materialismo, Posse, Começo.* Ganhos e prosperidade são tudo o que se avista no horizonte. Sorte e paz abençoarão o seu caminho.

2 DE OUROS — *Palavras-chave: Dualismo, Alegria, Flexibilidade, Irresponsabilidade, Inconstância.* A pressa é inimiga da perfeição. Se não consegue lidar com mais coisas ao mesmo tempo, abandone alguma delas antes de se prejudicar.

3 DE OUROS — *Palavras-chave: Artesanato, Arte, Projeto, Talento, Inspiração.* Avance com os seus projetos com paixão, mas planeie-os com atenção para não correr o risco de se prejudicar no processo.

4 DE OUROS — *Palavras-chave: Ganância, Parcimónia, Controlo, Herança, Investimento.* Proteger os seus próprios espaços é legítimo, mas o controlo possessivo e a ganância são atitudes das quais deve absolutamente manter-se afastado.

5 DE OUROS — *Palavras-chave: Necessidade, Pobreza, Luta, Obstáculo, Frieza.* Em momentos de escassez, virtudes como a generosidade e o respeito podem ajudá-lo a reerguer-se e tornar-se ainda mais forte do que antes.

6 DE OUROS — *Palavras-chave: Generosidade, Caridade, Distribuição, Empatia, Oferta.* O altruísmo exige sacrifícios, mas as recompensas serão sempre maiores do que qualquer coisa que tenha de ser sacrificada.

7 DE OUROS — *Palavras-chave: Avaliação, Expansão, Dever, Desenvolvimento, Controlo.* Pode parecer contraintuitivo, mas esperar pode ser o ato mais produtivo que existe. Não se apresse e deixe que as situações deem os seus frutos.

8 DE OUROS — *Palavras-chave: Trabalho, Hábito, Empenho, Autonomia, Precisão.* A dedicação a um objetivo é uma qualidade admirável: empenhe-se na sua ocupação ou paixão para alcançar o máximo e evitar futuros arrependimentos.

9 DE OUROS — *Palavras-chave: Prudência, Independência, Educação, Seguran-*

ça, Riqueza. Emancipação e independência são as diretrizes. As situações problemáticas serão resolvidas à medida que desenvolver habilidades secundárias para lidar com elas.

10 DE OUROS — *Palavras-chave: Riqueza, Herança, Vínculo, Topo, Casa.* Seja resiliente. A herança, as tradições e todas as transmissões de riquezas físicas ou imateriais são sintomas de uma continuidade saudável.

VALETE DE OUROS — *Palavras-chave: Esforço, Estudo, Praticidade, Curiosidade, Prova.* A curiosidade é algo positivo, mas é importante ter cuidado para não se deixar levar demais e não se esforçar excessivamente nos estudos ou no trabalho.

CAVALEIRO DE OUROS — *Palavras-chave: Adaptabilidade, Pragmatismo, Persistência, Profissionalismo, Confiabilidade.* Concentre-se e avance com a sua tarefa diligentemente para que tudo o que conquistou até agora não desapareça num instante.

REI DE OUROS — *Palavras-chave: Negócios, Empresa, Dinheiro, Administração, Maturação.* Assuma mais autoridade e responsabilidade ao avançar com os seus projetos, e em breve poderá colher os suculentos frutos do sucesso.

RAINHA DE OUROS — *Palavras-chave: Preservação, Consciência, Nutrimento, Coração, Discrição.* Por vezes são necessárias medidas severas para preservar o que tem valor. Cuide especialmente das coisas e das pessoas que lhe são queridas.

PAUS

ÁS DE PAUS — *Palavras-chave: Criatividade, Originalidade, Aventura, Força, Vivacidade.* Seja positiva ou negativa, esta é a faísca que dá início a uma nova aventura, à chama sagrada alimentada pela potência da criação.

2 DE PAUS — *Palavras-chave: Plano, Aspirações, Impulso, Agitação, Arrogância.* Os seus projetos beneficiam-se de uma preparação impecável, mas cuidado para não alimentar excessivamente as expectativas – a arrogância sempre se voltará contra si.

3 DE PAUS — *Palavras-chave: Antecipação, Observação, Atenção, Atraso, Previsão.* A pressa em perseguir um objetivo pode causar danos enormes. As coisas já estão em movimento: espere pelo momento certo para agir.

4 DE PAUS — *Palavras-chave: Celebração, Preparação, Tranquilidade, Perfeccionismo, Solidez.* Anuncia-se a chegada de um evento feliz, um momento para se alegrar com amigos e familiares ou simplesmente um encontro para restabelecer a estabilidade.

5 DE PAUS — *Palavras-chave: Competição, Rivalidade, Conflito, Treino, Imitação.* Uma competição saudável é certamente uma característica positiva, mas certifique-se de saber pelo que vale a pena lutar.

6 DE PAUS — *Palavras-chave: Vitoria, Fama, Vaidade, Diplomacia, Novidade.* Celebre o seu triunfo e não permita que ninguém estrague as celebrações, mas evite ser excessivamente meticuloso.

7 DE PAUS — *Palavras-chave: Defesa, Oposição, Opinião, Batalha, Anticonformis-*

mo. A batalha está próxima. Sinta-se livre para fazer a sua voz ser ouvida, mas esteja preparado para argumentar as suas afirmações com evidencias.

8 DE PAUS — *Palavras-chave: Velocidade, Movimento, Rapidez, Reação, Expedição.* Hesitar causa dor; a estagnação gera tristeza. Mantenha este pensamento em mente para perseguir os seus desafios com energia e rapidez.

9 DE PAUS — *Palavras-chave: Vigilância, Cautela, Persistência, Limiar, Experiência.* Algo ameaça o seu espaço pessoal, que deve vigiar com prudência. Cuidado, pois os perigos muitas vezes apresentam-se disfarçados de formas inofensivas.

10 DE PAUS — *Palavras-chave: Cansaço, Fadiga, Opressão, Exaustão, Conclusão.* É hora de se livrar do "peso morto" que carrega sobre os seus ombros. Pare de correr, pois o momento de descansar chegou.

VALETE DE PAUS — *Palavras-chave: Iniciativa, Vitalidade, Entusiasmo, Brincadeira, Risco.* Uma alma brincalhona e aventureira é algo extremamente benéfico.

Mas preste atenção: o seu fogo ainda é incipiente e representa uma defesa ineficaz contra os perigos no caminho.

CAVALEIRO DE PAUS — *Palavras-chave: Coragem, Impulso, Distância, Idealismo, Inconsciência.* Avance com determinação; atravesse o fogo para alcançar os seus objetivos. Se o que deseja estiver fora do alcance, não hesite em pedir ajuda para acelerar o passo.

REI DE PAUS — *Palavras-chave: Liderança, Motivação, Persuasão, Argúcia, Presunção.* A arrogância e a presunção podem colocá-lo em grandes riscos. Assuma as suas responsabilidades – afinal, é precisamente isso que um verdadeiro líder faz.

RAINHA DE PAUS — *Palavras-chave: Carisma, Magnetismo, Sensualidade, Otimismo, Vivacidade.* Combine delicadeza com agressividade – os pilares da personalidade carismática e multiforme que deve cultivar.

ESPADAS

ÁS DE ESPADAS — *Palavras-chave: Pensamento, Ideia, Objetividade, Responsabilidade, Convicção.* Supere os obstáculos com a força das novas ideias. Mas tenha cuidado, pois os pensamentos complicados podem levá-lo a uma disciplina excessivamente rígida e a responsabilidades desmedidas.

2 DE ESPADAS — *Palavras-chave: Duelo, Discussão, Dualismo, Impasse, Cegueira.* Escolha com sabedoria o percurso e os seus inimigos, e esteja atento às opções demasiadamente atraentes, pois a sua aparência pode esconder perigos imprevistos.

3 DE ESPADAS — *Palavras-chave: Desgosto, Dor, Desespero, Culpa, Remorso.* Um evento doloroso ou um antigo ressentimento bate agora à sua porta. Não se entregue ao desespero e enfrente o problema com coragem.

4 DE ESPADAS — *Palavras-chave: Recuperação, Sono, Trégua, Retiro, Pausa.* Não se torture com metas e ambições, pois a es-

tabilidade mental é fundamental. Conceda-se um tempo para descansar, refletir e recuperar-se.

5 DE ESPADAS — *Palavras-chave: Egoísmo, Satisfação, Dominação, Vingança, Drama.* Abandone o egoísmo, o orgulho e o desejo de poder. Seja humilde e esteja aberto à ajuda externa, se necessário, e o seu reino poderá finalmente ver a luz.

6 DE ESPADAS — *Palavras-chave: Viagem, Fuga, Renúncia, Expediente, Mudança.* Encontra-se entre a partida e o destino. Sentir-se à deriva é comum durante uma jornada, mas logo avistará a terra no horizonte.

7 DE ESPADAS — *Palavras-chave: Furtividade, Artimanhas, Engano, Espionagem, Acumulação.* Uma ameaça silenciosa aproxima-se; alguém mente ou faz pela calada. Ou talvez seja necessário recorrer as mesmas artimanhas para superar o problema.

8 DE ESPADAS — *Palavras-chave: Limite, Letargia, Inércia, Armadilha, Obstáculo.* Encontra-se numa situação de estagnação, possivelmente devido a um trauma passado. Partilhar este fardo poderia ser a chave para superar o bloqueio.

9 DE ESPADAS — *Palavras-chave: Angústia, Desespero, Incerteza, Trevas, Dúvida.* Está a experienciar dúvidas repentinas, sensação de culpa, ansiedades ou comportamentos obsessivos. Fale abertamente sobre este problema para livrar-se da energia negativa.

10 DE ESPADAS — *Palavras-chave: Aflição, Bloqueio, Sofrimento, Medo, Fim.* Não se apegue às lembranças de um passado que não retornará. Não se desespere: a perda não é nada além do prelúdio da transcendência.

VALETE DE ESPADAS — *Palavras-chave: Impaciência, Inteligência, Génio, Cálculo, Ajuda.* Mantenha-se atento e proteja o que deseja com astúcia, mas lembre-se de olhar além do seu perímetro para aprender mais e aprimorar-se.

CAVALEIRO DE ESPADAS — *Palavras-chave: Destreza, Impaciência, Valor, Pressa, Fraqueza.* Reflita antes de agir e tome decisões louváveis. Ser astuto e impaciente pode levá-lo a tirar conclusões precipitadas, às vezes.

REI DE ESPADAS — *Palavras-chave: Racionalidade, Análise, Precisão, Tática, Concentração.* Afirme-se e busque uma maneira de assumir o controlo da situação atual. Se confrontar alguém próximo for a única solução lógica, não hesite.

RAINHA DE ESPADAS — *Palavras-chave: Transparência, Estratégia, Rigor, Concisão, Disciplina.* As suas ações devem ser rápidas e diretas. Abra os lábios apenas para favorecer aqueles que o merecem ou punir os indignos, sem deixar nada a meio caminho.